SPARTANBURG PEOPLE'S COURT

The History of Spartanburg County Magistrate's Court

James B. Paslay

Cover by Heather Walters

Drawings by James B. Paslay

Copyright © 2022 James B. Paslay

All rights reserved.

ISBN-13: 9798773899204

Dedication

The magistrate court could not have existed without good staff members and constables. These people worked very hard and long hours many times. They had to deal with many angry people and help people who needed just to understand the system. They did this extremely well.

The men and women who served as judges both in the district courts and at the courthouse also worked long hours often late at night, on week-ends, and holidays. Most of these judges performed very well and deserve the credit for making Spartanburg's magistrate court the best in the state.

The senators supported our courts extremely well and I appreciate them appointing me for the forty-five years I served. Two senators were extremely supportive and fully understood how important it was to have judges all through the county. They fought efforts to close regional offices because they knew it would deny the people they represented easier access to solve their problems. These two senators were Horace Smith and Glenn Reese and they deserve recognition for their support of the court.

Especially helpful in the creation of this book was the staff of the South Carolina Department of Archives and History in Columbia. These people went out of their way to supply the list of judges and the dates of their appointments since 1785.

Robert "Bob" Paslay interviewed several of the prominent judges in the book and edited the book. His experience as a newspaper reporter, writer and editor was extremely valuable.

* * *

Table of Contents

Chapter 1 – What? Me a Judge? 1
Chapter 2 – Early Evolution of Office of Magistrate 5
Chapter 3 – Early Settlement of South Carolina 11
Chapter 4 – The Sptbg. District Magistrates and Freeholders Court 25
Chapter 5 – Dark Days and the Renewal 31
Chapter 6 – The Tillman Era and the Early 20th Century 38
Chapter 7 – The Selection of Magistrates 42
Chapter 8 – The Battle Over Magistrate Appointments 50
Chapter 9 – The City of Spartanburg Magistrates 60
Chapter 10 – The Creation of the Chief Magistrate 83
Chapter 11 – Surrender those Civil Rights 91
Chapter 12 – Community standards 93
Chapter 13 – Types of cases heard 99
Chapter 14 – How magistrates are paid 106
Chapter 15 – The People 110
Chapter 16 – Sptbg's Most Influential Magistrates in Modern Times 115
Chapter 17 – The Dark Side: Misconduct by Magistrates 144
Chapter 18 – Conclusion 153
Appendix 1 157
Appendix 2 Quorum 162
Appendix 3 Mags 1800 165
Appendix 4 Mags 1841 174
Appendix 5 Mags 1900 182
Appendix 6 Courthouses 196
Bibliography 202

Preface

I owe my career as a magistrate for the past forty five years to some very influential females in my life. The first was my mother, Agnes H. Paslay, who was a strong, smart and wise woman. She was unusual in the 1940's as a working woman outside the home. Most women in this era were homemakers with no other career. My mother was a homemaker and a professional woman.

She had a love for the law, being married to a second generation lawyer. Her career as a staff member in the magistrate court spanned over thirty-five years. During that time, she learned of an opening as night and weekend magistrate. Single handedly, she campaigned for me for this position and launched my entry into the profession.

Upon my appointment, I met the second influential female in my life, Judge Ellen Hines Smith. Judge Smith was also a smart and wise woman in a man's profession. At the time, female judges were viewed as interlopers into the legal profession. They were often treated with disdain and had to endure some humiliating treatment by their peers. Ellen Smith handled the challenge with a calm and highly professional demeanor. She became a true role model for females who later followed her into the legal profession. For me, she was a valuable mentor. We both suffered different types of prejudice. For me at age twenty-seven, it was age prejudice. Often upon meeting me for the first time, people had no problem pronouncing "You are too young to be a judge!" .

The third female who impacted my life was Karen Kanes (later Karen Kanes Floyd). After several years on the job, I had lost some of the drive I had once had to take on challenges with overwhelming odds. Karen came onto the court, soon convincing the chief justice to make her the chief magistrate, even though she was the least experienced judge on the court. That same drive got her elected as an administrative law judge, the Chairman of Spartanburg County Council, and the Chair of the State Republican Party. She had an ambition and an energy level that made you want to work harder and attempt challenges you might never have considered.

The final female who influenced me perhaps to the largest degree was a young woman named Fran Bowen. I believe I fell in love with her the moment I first met her. As my partner for more than fifty-two years, she has stood beside me in good times and bad. She is smart, wise and politically savvy. With Karen Kanes' inspiration and Fran Paslay's work ethic I became a better judge and the chief magistrate. However, I would never have taken on the challenges without the influence of these strong, wise and intelligent women. I would have forever regretted had I not tried.

This book is a tribute to the outstanding men and women who have served as magistrates in Spartanburg County. It is also a reflection of the influence on the history of the legal profession that many of these people have exerted.

***

INTRODUCTION or What this Book Isn't

The book you are holding is not a legal textbook. It was never meant to be. Therefore, you will not find formal legal citations to cases. When cases are referred to, enough information is given so that if you go to a law library, with a little help from the librarian, you can find the actual case. This book is a history book, but, although I was a history major in college, it may not follow all the precise formatting in citing sources that a professor of history might use. This book is a book for laymen.

This book was written for several reasons. Firstly, there was no book that addressed the subject which I believe is very important to a lot of people. Because the magistrate court is not a court of record, cases heard are not recorded in formal legal volumes. Often, what is known of the decisions is reported in the local press. But as with most reporters of things legal, the authors of such articles often are not versed in the law, resulting sometimes in lack of understanding of the importance of decisions made in the courts. Hopefully, this book may serve to correct or illuminate some of those issues more clearly.

The second reason I decided to write the book is because I was asked to – dozens of times. People knew I had served for a long time and would ask, "How did you used to do this?" Sometimes the request was "tell me about some of your most interesting cases." Most importantly, the question was "How have you survived these many years as a judge when others have not?" The answer to the last question, I believe, is that my parents instilled in me and my siblings a code of behavior to care for others that has guided my life. That is the best answer I can give, however, this book might expand on this a bit further.

I don't expect this book to land on The New York Times best seller list. However, many people who have learned that the book was being written have indicated a desire for a copy. For some, they may be hoping they do not show up in a bad light. I hope that does not happen, and, with guidance of my brother Bob, who is an experienced newsman, both as reporter and editor, I have tried to avoid the libel suit. That does not mean that controversial issues were avoided. These are part of the story of the development of the court. In writing about them we have endeavored to be fair at all times.

My brother, Robert D. Paslay, known as "Robbie" to his family and "Bob" to his fellow newsmen and associates, was an English major at Wofford College. He, like my whole family, has had an interest in history and law. He has served as a reporter and editor for newspapers all along the East Coast. His skills of interviewing and writing have been invaluable. He interviewed as many people as possible who had interesting stories to tell. After reading my first two chapters, he said "this is too dry." I hope with his help we have made the story more readable.

Since this is a history book, the events that led to the development of our "people's court" must be seen in the context of what was happening . Accordingly, we have relied heavily on some of Spartanburg County's best historians to paint that picture. These include A.O. Landrum, Dr. Lewis P. Jones, Vernon Foster, and Professor Phillip Racine, who have written excellent books about the development of Spartanburg County. These are listed in the credits in the back of this book.

This book takes that background and attempts to show how a court to serve the people developed and why it developed the way it did. I think the story is fascinating . I have been proud to be a part of it for forty-five years – longer than any other fulltime magistrate in Spartanburg history. Maybe the book in the end simply is me exhaling after holding so many thoughts inside for this long.

Lots of people have asked me about their relatives that they believed were magistrates. With the help of the South Carolina Department of Archives and History in Columbia, I have been able to list most of the magistrates (earlier called Justices of the Peace and Justices of the Quorum) who served in our county from the beginning to the present. You will find them in the back of the book. The date appointed and the date confirmed is given as often as possible. Sometimes I could only find the date of confirmation.

Stories of some of the most influential magistrates are given to show the value of the people who served in these offices and the challenges they faced making many difficult decisions. Hopefully you will find this interesting and it will give you a greater appreciation for the difficult tasks these judges face daily.

CHAPTER ONE

Chapter 1 - What? Me a Judge

The phone rang startling me awake at two in the morning. A voice on the other end said, " I am Detective Sawyer. I understand you have been appointed a new judge. I need to get an arrest warrant." For just a moment I was dazed. Then I replied, " I was appointed but have not received my commission or been sworn in. " After hanging up, my darling pregnant wife turned to me and asked, " Is this the way it is going to be?"

And so it was. At age twenty-seven, I was the youngest judge to have been appointed in Spartanburg County history at the time. My responsibilities were nights, week-ends and holidays. My duty schedule was working from 5:00 p.m. until midnight during the week and then being on call until 8:30 a.m. the following morning. On weekends, I was on duty or on call from 5:00 p.m. Friday night until 8:30 a.m. the following Monday. I was allowed Tuesday night off.

Since the judge who was to cover for me on Tuesday night disappeared at 7:00 p.m., if I had not taken my phone off the hook on Tuesday night I might never have fathered another child. Even with this, narcotic agents would often shine a flashlight in my bedroom window in the early morning hours of my night off. I always accommodated them.

As a fulltime judge of the Civil and Criminal Court, I was paid for thirty-seven and one-half hours per week as approved for fulltime employees of Spartanburg County. I actually worked easily twice that amount of time. However, this was the job I took, so I never complained. It amused me when other judges who received an hourly wage complained about working an extra fifteen minutes and not being paid for it.

I never set out to be a judge. At a very early age, as a fan of the television series "Perry Mason" and with both a father and grandfather as lawyers, I knew that I wanted to be a lawyer. Additionally, my mother had worked as a clerk in the magistrate court for over twenty-five years. Both of my parents had a profound love for the law and instilled that in their children.

This is the main reason at the beginning of my last semester at Wofford College, that I applied to go to law school at the University of South Carolina. When I told my father of my plans, he encouraged me to go to medical school. After sticking to my guns, I am sure he was proud that I chose this course.

Law school was a brand new challenge unlike anything else I had done. There were no tests or means of measuring what you had learned until the end of the semester. Final exams consisted of about four factual questions for which each student was issued a blue essay book. The object was to identify and discuss the legal issues posed by the facts and reach a conclusion. Grades were issued based on how well the issues were explored or identified. There were no specific right or wrong answers.

As mentioned earlier, the main reason I chose to go to law school was the influence of my parents. However, there was another significant factor. At Wofford College, I was in the Reserve Officer Training Corps (ROTC). As such, I was due to be commissioned as a second lieutenant in the U.S. Army Reserve upon my graduation. At the beginning of the second semester in 1968, the North Vietnamese began an incursion into the South known as the Tet Offensive.

The Vietnam War was raging and the Tet Offensive made it even hotter. Second lieutenants in the Army had a life expectancy in Vietnam of about thirty minutes. This became a major consideration for my application to law school. I received one of the few remaining deferments from entering military service to enter law school. As a consequence, I had a strong incentive to stay in school.

This incentive translated into living in the law library. I studied long and hard and joined a group of other first year students for joint study sessions and brain storming. At the time there were many first year students who had graduated from The Citadel. The Citadel for those readers who don't know is a military academy. Each weekend these alumni would return to The Citadel for various parties and celebrations. I spent my weekends in the law library.

When the first exam blue books were given out, after about twenty minutes, a parade began of The Citadel grads as they one by one turned in their blue books. Since I knew their destination, I bore down harder and wrote like the wind, filling my blue book with my discussion of the issues. Even so, it was very unnerving waiting for the results of those exams. It was halfway through the second semester that the grades were posted. They were posted by the student's social security number and I repeated this over in my head as I approached the board bearing the grades. One by one I breathed a sigh of relief as I realized I was on my way to another year of law school.

The law school experience was exciting and enjoyable for me. My fiancée and I were married just before the beginning of my second year and Fran Bowen and I began a life filled with challenges and rewards. She would visit me in the musty stacks of the law library on Saturday afternoon. We learned to take full advantage of the few times we had together. I think she believed it would all be worth it when I became a rich and famous lawyer. She had no idea we would be getting those two in the morning calls at that time.

Because I did well in school, I had many opportunities offered to me. But I did not want to be an errand boy in a large law firm. I wanted to actually practice law. As a result, I came back and joined a law firm that had been doing that since 1902 in Spartanburg. In 1971, I became a new partner in the firm of Paslay and Paslay, Attorneys at Law.

For the next two years, I appeared in every court in Spartanburg. Our general practice of law went from bankruptcies to criminal defense. I appeared often in the Civil and Criminal Court. This court was a hybrid type court – having magistrate level criminal jurisdiction but with civil jurisdiction greater than the magistrate court. Judges of the court had to be attorneys.

For many years prior to the creation of the Civil and Criminal Court, magistrates had served at the courthouse. These "courthouse magistrates" were attorneys and because they served a heavily populated area, had a larger caseload that the average magistrate. My mother worked for these judges and I remember Judge Ralph Mitchell and Judge Bobo Burnett as I visited my mother in a little building that stood in the middle of what is now the parking lot of the County Judicial Center.

In the mid 1950's, the courthouse magistrates became the nucleus of the Spartanburg Civil Court , which was a misnomer since the court handled both civil and criminal matters. The Spartanburg Civil Court became the Spartanburg Civil and Criminal Court in 1970. The court had two daytime judges and one Night and Weekend Judge. One of the judges was appointed as the Chief Judge of the court. The first Judge to hold the nighttime position was Judge Wallace Dickerson. He was uniquely suited for this job, since he also volunteered as a rescue squad operator. The rescue squad was a type of volunteer ambulance service, so Judge Dickerson was used to being called at all hours to carry out this mission.

In 1973, Judge Dickerson was moved to first shift to fill a vacancy, leaving his position open. I got a call from my mother who said she had been asked by Senator Horace Smith if she knew someone who might want this job. She recommended me and she called me to ask if I had an interest. As a young lawyer, income was sporadic and sometimes fees were hard to collect. The $12,000 annual salary was good for the time, and the job included medical insurance. So I agreed to be a candidate. In the end, apparently, no one else was intrigued by the long and difficult hours so I became the sacrificial lamb.

Over the next nearly forty-five years, Fran and I began a journey that we could never have imagined. There were, of course, good times and bad. This is the story of a court system and the responses to an ever changing society. The court evolved as did the surrounding community and at all times provided a means to resolve disputes in a calm and safe atmosphere. Such is the role of the people's courts which we know officially as the magistrate court.

This court did not just spring up. As a matter of fact, it developed over a long time into the court of today. To understand this development, we must go back in time to when our state was first settled and see the story unfold as part of the history of our state. The journey begins in the next chapter.

CHAPTER TWO

Chapter 2 - Early Evolution of Office of Magistrate

The basis of most of the laws of early South Carolina arose from the mother country of England. Wars and periods of upheaval were common in England for centuries. Kings were overthrown in wars and insurrections. Oftentimes other countries, particularly France and Spain, played roles in overthrowing regimes and choosing kings more loyal to their interests.

With this unsettled environment, many villages wanted to be left alone to live in peace. Accordingly, they began electing keepers of the peace who became known as "justices of the peace." These officers often only served during times of crisis. No specific duties were assigned other than the authority to keep the peace.

In the year 1327, with the help of his mother and one Edward Mortimer, at the age of fourteen years, Edward III, forced his father from the throne and became King of England. For years Mortimer was the de facto king until Edward wrestled the throne away. Edward III, began to instill a sense of law and order to the country. During his reign, the Parliament evolved and other institutions of government were established.

Justices of the Peace were established and were appointed by the king. These officers were established by acts of Parliament in each county with the authority to "hear and determine felonies and trespasses done in the said counties, and to inflict punishment reasonably, according to the law and reason and the manner of the deed."

There were two classes of justices established - justices of the peace and justices of the quorum. Justices of the Peace were to "enforce and punish offences against the Statutes made for the quiet and natural government of the realm." Justices of the Quorum were more "learned in the law" and had all the powers of their brethren but had additional authority to try all offences "other than mere breaches of the peace."

Gradually the authority of justices of the peace was enlarged by statutes which empowered justices of the peace to cause to be arrested and bound over to the higher court those that committed serious offences. Peace judges could also commit to bail most people who were to appear in the higher court. Additionally, justices of the peace were required to sit with the justices of the quorum four times a year when court was conducted.

As England began to explore and colonize, it established early settlements in the West Indies, particularly on the Island of Barbados. These islands south of Florida and near the island of Cuba, developed a culture in which slave labor became the means to cultivate the agricultural products desired by the mother country. Additionally, the settlements developed a system of laws based on English common law but uniquely suited to the needs of the colonial lifestyle.

Accordingly, Barbados enacted a series of "slave codes" which prescribed the relationship of everyone to the slave community. These codes were designed to ensure peace and tranquility between the free population and that of the enslaved population. Offenses were established as well as punishments for these offenses.

Early settlement of the province of South Carolina in Charles Town was an outgrowth of the provinces of the West Indies. Most immigrants to the South Carolina province came from Barbados. Accordingly, much of the culture on the coast was taken from the island. This included the laws that were developed in the West Indies and included the system of justices of the peace and quorum. In 1690, the South Carolina provincial assembly adopted the slave codes from Barbados. Slaves violating the law were to be tried by two justices of the peace and three freeholders. This system was the forerunner of the Magistrates and Freeholders Courts discussed in more detail in another chapter.

Author Edward McCrady, in his book "The history of South Carolina under the proprietary government, 1670-1719", published in 1897 by the MacMillen Company, opined that though the slave codes were harsh, they were no more severe than the punishments provided to white freemen in England at the time. A sailor that struck his commander was summarily put to death. According to the author, "The scheme of the court of Justices and Freeholders was taken also from the Barbadian Act. And in regard to that statute it was observed that the form of trial it provided was in all respects competent to the administration of justice, 'and candid men,' continues the author just quoted 'may think that a tribunal consisting of two magistrates and three jurymen may be as capable of deciding justly as the military and naval courts martial which are allowed to decide upon the laws of freemen.'"

As time went on, the colonial legislature, and later the state legislature, amended the structure to meet the needs of the times. In 1686 an act was passed granting justices of the peace authority over small claims for debt. This amount was set at twenty dollars by 1799. An act passed in 1740 granted authority to justices of the peace to try and punish, if convicted, free people of color and slaves for any violations of law. This act expanded the authority already in place and amended some of the slave codes.

An act of 1839, effective March 1, 1841, abolished the office of justice of the quorum and renamed justices of the peace as magistrates. Justices of the peace had long since been freed from the obligation to sit with justices of the quorum for trials. The act creating magistrates provided that they were to be appointed by both houses of the legislature for a term of four years, and to extend for forty days after the end of the session of the legislature, at which time the terms would expire. Vacancies could be appointed by the Governor but would extend only to the end of the next session of the legislature.

By 1848, a new act provided that there would be one magistrate for each "beat company" and two for each corporate town and courthouse village. A person appointed as magistrate could not own a tavern or a license to sell spirituous liquors. Neither could members of his household or relatives. A person convicted of violating this provision was forever barred from serving as a magistrate.

Prior to this act, there was no limit on the amount of bail a magistrate could set for one accused of a crime. This act set maximum bail amounts but prohibited excessive bail. Generally, the maximum bail was the maximum amount of the fine that could be imposed upon conviction. Statutory maximum bail amounts for gambling and killing a slave were $500.00 each.

There was no provision for appeal from convictions in magistrate criminal cases except for conviction of a capital case (cases involving the death penalty). Since magistrates could only hear capital cases involving slaves and persons of color, a provision existed for a motion for a new trial filed with a circuit judge or judge of the court of appeals. If the motion was granted, the case was sent to a different magistrate than the original trial magistrate for the new trial.

In this same era, South Carolina established the Magistrates and Freeholders Courts which will be explored more fully in another chapter. Unfortunately , by the year 1846, the South Carolina Senate had become aware of the lack of training of magistrates, resulting in non uniform applications of the law throughout the state. As a result, a resolution was passed by the South Carolina Senate on December 18, 1846, which read as follows:

" **The Committee on District Offices, to whom was referred a Resolution to authorize the Governor to cause a compilation of laws and decisions of the Court of Appeals, relative to the duties and powers of Magistrates and Constables, have had the same under consideration and beg leave to Report: That they cannot, in their opinion, too strongly impress upon the House, the necessity of such a work as the said resolution contemplates. -That the Magistrates and Constables are, in a large majority of the cases, ignorant of the laws which the Legislature makes it their duty to enforce ,does not admit of a doubt. These laws are now dispensed over many thousands of pages of law books, which are to them, in great measure, wholly inaccessible, and being thus deficient in the knowledge of the laws which is their duty to enforce, and having no means within their power to obtain that knowledge, they must, of necessity, be wanting in that confidence in their own ability, without which it is vain to expect an efficient discharge of their duties."**

The resolution went on to recommend that the Governor be given authority to commission a knowledgeable person to compile the laws and case decisions into a format understandable by the magistrates and constables and to be published and distributed to them. The resolution passed and the governor commissioned one B.C. Pressley of the Charleston Bar to perform this task. This resulted in the publication of "The Law of Magistrates and Constables in the State of South Carolina" in 1848 by the publishing house of Walker and Burke.

Much of the history of the magistrate court related above was culled from this excellent work. The book is a treatise on the laws as they existed at the time of publication. This included criminal and civil procedure, explaining the standards for arrest and search warrants. Similar books were published over time, and today's guide is the "Bench Book for Magistrates" published for several years by the Office of Court Administration.

Pressley's book is out of print but fortunately it is available in digital format through the Amazon.com bookstore as a Google online book. Reading through the crimes that existed at the time provides an interesting picture of the culture of the time. Vagrancy was a major concern. The old adage that "idol hands are the devil's workshop" seemed to apply. Persons who had no visible means of support who simply hung around were viewed with great suspicion. Accordingly, anyone could bring a complaint to the magistrate accusing a person of vagrancy.

If a complaint was filed, the magistrate would cause the person accused to be brought before him to be examined as to conduct. The magistrate could require them to post a bond to ensure good behavior. If the person could not post the bond, he would be arrested and bound over for trial in the higher court.

Many offenses appear in the book as the statutes at the time setting out the relationship between whites and slaves. An overview of the culture of the time clearly can be constructed from these laws. It was unlawful for anyone to whip a slave without a justifiable reason. Upon conviction, the defendant could be sentenced to six months in jail. Additionally, selling liquor to slaves, teaching a slave to read and write, or engaging in games of chance with a slave were criminal offenses.

The guidebook on the law of magistrates set forth the procedures for issuing arrest warrants, for setting bail, and for binding over offenders to the higher court for trial. It contained forms and examples of the documents magistrates were to complete to carry out their responsibilities under the laws that existed. Although this was a step in the right direction, no requirements for magistrates to receive any formal training in the law would be made for nearly another century and a half.

CHAPTER THREE
Chapter 3 - Early Settlement of South Carolina

The early history of South Carolina saw several failed attempts by the Spanish and French explorers to colonize what is now our state. In the mid seventeenth century, with the help of a group of English noblemen known as the Lords Proprietors, Charles II became the King of England. As a reward, he gave the Proprietors a land grant of the Carolinas. These people saw the new world as a place to enrich themselves, so they outfitted three ships to sail to their newly acquired land.

In 1670, one of the three ships arrived near what is now Charleston and established a settlement which they named for the king as Charles Towne. By 1703, the population of the new village had grown to eight thousand, with half being slaves. Illness was so prevalent, that the village became known as "sick town". Fires often destroyed the wooden houses and buildings and attacks by Indians and pirates were frequent. Pleas to the Proprietors for help fell on deaf ears, so the people had to fend off these threats themselves. In spite of these challenges, Charles Towne prospered and was the seat of government for the new colony for over a hundred years.

In 1897, one Edward McCrady, a Charleston lawyer and vice president of the South Carolina Historical Society, wrote "The History of South Carolina under the proprietary government, 1670-1719" which was published by the MacMillen Company. Two years later he wrote "The History of South Carolina under the royal government,

1719-1776" which was also published by the MacMillen Company. These two works trace the development of South Carolina's law and courts from the founding of the colony until the American Revolution.

McCrady points out that the colony of South Carolina was unique among the British colonies because it was separated by both distance and geography from the colonies of Virginia and New England to the north. Additionally, it was threatened by the Spanish to the south and the French to the north and the Indians inland. Pirates were a regular threat. As a result of this, for the first hundred years, the settlement of the colony did not reach far outside of the Charles Towne area.

Government was focused in Charleston until 1790 when it moved to Columbia. There were no county or township governments until after the Civil War. Every magistrate in the province was appointed in Charleston until 1776. For protection, the province was divided into military districts and these were further divided into "beat districts" which were patrolled by a police captain.

Although the courts were patterned upon the system of England, they were adapted to the local needs and were not as many or as complex. Courts consisted of a Court of Common Pleas or Supreme Court of Charleston, as it was often known, presided over by a Chief Justice and four assistants, and the Court of General Sessions, for the trial of all offenses punishable by death, presided over by the Chief Justice, or, in his absence, any two assistants.

Although some were, there was no requirement that the Chief Justice be a lawyer. None of the assistants were ever lawyers nor were the early magistrates. Only the Chief Justice received compensation. The lower judges served because it was a title of honor but were never paid. The Chief Justice was appointed from officials in England, but the Proprietors or the Royal Governor appointed the assistants and the magistrates. While many of these judges served with honor and skill, quite a few did not. The offices were most often delivered to repay favors done for the Proprietors or the King.

One such example was the appointment of Charles Shinner as Chief Justice in 1762. McCrady describes him as follows: "Shinner was an Irishman of the lowest class, with no better education than is usually given to qualify one for the meanest mechanical trade." However, through a series of good fortunes he obtained a job transporting documents back and forth between the courts of England and Ireland. He came to render a service to a lady who was engaged in a lawsuit in Ireland who happened to be the mistress of a powerful Englishman, Lord Halifax. Upon her recommendation, Lord Halifax appointed Shinner as Chief Justice for South Carolina.

Such offices in the colonies were looked upon by the gentry in England as favors to be handed out. They did not care who presided over the local laws in the colonies. However, McCrady wrote that Halifax first tried to find a position for Shinner in England but found " the vulgar, illiterate ignoramus unfit for any place of credit at home.." Accordingly, Skinner ascended to the highest judicial office in the colony.

In 1767, a committee of the Colonial Assembly of South Carolina was appointed to study the state of the courts. The committee's conclusion was that the honorable Chief Justice was "a person wholly unacquainted with the common law, acts of Parliament, or acts of the Assembly of the province; that his conduct manifested such ignorance as to show him utterly unfit for a place of so much consequence.."

As examples of the jurist's behavior the report cited an instance where Shinner had caused to be arrested without a warrant a wagoner who had smacked his whip while passing the Chief Justice's carriage, frightening his honor's horse. In another instance, Skinner delivered a man to jail at the point of a gun without a warrant alleging he had threatened a female acquaintance of the judge. To cover up the matter, Shinner told the jailer to abduct the defendant and ship him out on the next available vessel and to blame a local lawyer for the entire affair. The jailer refused to lie and the truth was told.

Finally, the report found that the judge routinely used vile and profane language in court and insulted those that appeared before him. He also took great joy in attending executions of those who had sentenced to death and engaged in drunken rabble rousing with the assembled mobs in taunting the convicted person. Shinner was ultimately removed from his office by the Governor but cited in his defense that the reason for his behavior was his ignorance of the law.

The author McCrady concluded that by 1775 that there were only 35 members of the bar in South Carolina. However, there were many influential members who had been trained in the law in

England like Charles Pinckney and John Rutledge. These and others who wished to develop a strong court system with well trained judges who adhered to the law helped lead the colony towards a desire to separate from the mother country.

These individuals argued that within the law, the colony should have a greater right to decide the laws that govern them and provide their rights and privileges. Judges should be appointed with a goal of providing justice and not to enrich the King. Finally, under the law, people should not have to endure oppressive taxes raised without them having representation in the governing bodies who impose those duties. Accordingly, McCrady concluded that these young and influential lawyers helped turn the feelings of the people toward the desire to be free and independent from England.

DEVELOPMENT OF THE UPSTATE BEGINS

For reasons cited earlier, the development of the inland and upstate areas of South Carolina was delayed for almost a hundred years from the founding of the colony. A treaty signed by Royal Governor James Glenn with the Cherokee Indians in 1755 helped calm hostilities within the colony. Prior to this treaty, only the most daring individuals ventured far beyond the confines of the coastline. It was simply not safe to do so. However, three classes of people began to explore the interior of the state many years before settlements began.

First there was the hunter. He had no desire to settle, cultivate or expand civilization. He was a loner who developed great skill with a rifle. This impressed the native Indians and began the process of interacting between white man and Indians. Next came the cow driver, who again impressed the Indians with his self reliance and hardy spirit.

The cow drivers set up cow pens, which were the beginnings of small villages. A cow pen consisted of several log cabins next to the enclosures for the livestock. A large clearing in the forest was made where corn was cultivated. When everyone was home and the cattle were in their enclosures, this presented a noisy civilized scene in the middle of a savage wilderness.

The final group which predated the formal settlements was the Indian trader. These people gave up the comforts of life to endure an austere existence to trade trinkets with the Indians for furs and skins that brought a good return back in Charles Towne. Evidence exists that this hardy souls ventured along Indian trails well into the interior of the province prior to 1700 – while Charles Towne was still in its infancy.

Expansion into the Back Country

The early pioneers into the back country had no desire to create settlements, thus they created no threat to the native Indians. In 1730, however, Governor Robert Johnson introduced a township plan for the interior. The idea was to encourage the settlement of several frontier townships. These settlements would serve several purposes. The one desired most was to have a buffer that would protect Charleston from threats of runaway slaves or slave revolts. By this time, there were twice as many slaves in the low country as free whites. The governor believed that the townships would discourage runaway slaves and that the inhabitants would assist the low country in the event of a slave revolt.

The new townships were few in number and only were established up to about the area of present day Columbia. However, in the 1740's and 1750's pioneers began to settle into the upstate in areas known as the Long Canes and Ninety Six, just south of present Spartanburg County. Shortly thereafter, pioneering settlers began to settle in what is now Spartanburg County.

Along what is the present border with North Carolina and down into what is now Pickens, Oconee, Cherokee and Spartanburg Counties was a nation of Cherokee Indians. Clashes occurred between the settlers and the Cherokees, which limited the development of the region. However, since the settlers were few and the other white inhabitants were traders, hunters and cowboys, relative calm remained among the whites and their Indian neighbors.

By 1755, Governor Glenn's treaty with the Indians opened up the upstate districts for settlement, returning Spartanburg and twelve other upstate districts to English rule. The relations with the Proprietors and the King had deteriorated. Also in 1755, the French were engaged with a war with the English colonies and England which was known as "the French and Indian War". This was because the French explorers had befriended the local Indians and worked with them to drive out a common enemy – the new colonists. In that year, in what is now Pittsburgh, Pennsylvania, the French, with the aid of the Indian allies, attacked and captured a trading outpost called

Fort Duquesne. The colonists appealed to England for help. In response, Major General Edward Braddock led a force (which included George Washington, Daniel Boone, and Daniel Morgan) in an effort to recapture Fort Duquesne.

Braddock was poorly trained to fight Indians, resulting in his force being ambushed. Two-thirds of his army was killed or captured. Many more were severely tortured. The word of the massacre spread quickly, and many of the Scotch-Irish settlers in the Pennsylvania region began to migrate south. They hacked out a trail that became known as the Great Philadelphia Wagon Road over which traveled oxen and wagons into what is now known as the upstate of South Carolina.

Elijah Clarke is believed to be the first Spartanburg County resident, settling in what is now Clifton in 1755. He stayed only about ten years before moving on. A group of Pennsylvania Scotch-Irish families followed and by 1766 permanent settlements had been established. Life was rough in these communities. Shelter was described by observers of the time as less substantial than the Indian tee -pees. Log cabins did pop up but were miles apart. Disease was rampant, wild animals were threatening, and skirmishes with the native Indians were common.

A common thread uniting the sparsely populated area of about twenty square miles that would form the nucleus of Spartanburg County was a common religion. The Calvinist Presbyterians that had migrated down from Pennsylvania met in each other 's cabins. Religion became the guiding force for residents, providing what social interaction they had. The strict principles of the Calvinists also established the law for the newly forming communities. No judicial officers existed in the upcountry at this time, even though the governor did appoint magistrates for each of the colony's districts, no records can be found of magistrates serving in the Spartan District in these early days. In 1769, circuit courts were established for the whole state and the first court held in the Spartan District was in 1772.

Most justice was vigilante in nature and was swift and vicious. Survival of the fittest, as defined by Charles Darwin, reigned supreme. The circuit courts only met once a year, and only in Charles Town, and not many were willing to wait that long for settling the issues with those that committed crimes. So lynchings were frequent as were other forms of mutilations and branding that would say to the world that "you are looking at a thief!". People had little time to take arrested persons to Charles Towne for trials. Even when they did, the Royal Governors would often pardon convicted criminals.

However, in 1759, Glenn's treaty became strained as the Cherokees began to fear continued expansion of white settlers into their nation. Thus began a series of attacks by the Indians on local settlements in the northernmost portion of the back country. One such attack occurred in early 1760 as a group of settlers left the Long Canes area to seek safety in nearby Georgia. About forty settlers, mostly women and children, were killed or captured. One of the party was Patrick Calhoun, father of John C. Calhoun, who escaped the ambush. His wife, unfortunately, was slain in the attack. Calhoun returned to the site a few days later to find only twenty inhumanely butchered bodies.

The settlers began to create a series of forts which were really just large farms around which stockades were constructed. The settlers entered these forts and remained there for the most part for the next two years. Between the Indians and bands of outlaws which included runaway slaves, vagrants, and misfits , the countryside of the back country was devastated. The inhabitants of the forts could not venture forth to tend their lands or protect their livestock. Finally, the Governor sent groups of Rangers into the area and defeated the Cherokees. The Indians were no longer a threat to the settlers.

When the settlers attempted to take back their lands, many found them occupied by the outlaws and misfits that had devastated the economy during the Cherokee War. The area was a lawless frontier similar to what we see in the many movies of the Wild, Wild West. No courts existed and the only judicial officers were justices of the peace and their constables. The justices of the peace at that time had no criminal jurisdiction.

The backcountry was allotted very few seats in the House of Commons which was the lower house of the South Carolina legislature. Accordingly, the area had very little political influence. Pleas were made to the government to provide courts to the interior, but much resistance to this existed in the royal government in the mother country of England.

In his book "The South Carolina Regulators", published in 1963 by the Belnap Press, Richard Maxwell Brown described the state of justice at the time "The justices of the peace were the most important men in the Back Country. Their judicial power was slight, but they performed a number of other duties. They 'issued warrants of the peace and warrants of hue and cry, administered oaths, took depositions, attested the returns of appraisements, and issued certificates for the heads of wild beasts, so that the owner could get his bounty.' One of their most important duties was that of toll master, wherein they 'took charge of stray livestock, advertised for the owners, and, if they were unclaimed, sold them for the benefit of the public and the informers.'"

"The importance of the justice of the peace became apparent on Saturday, the day he held his sittings. The Back Country then came alive. A carnival atmosphere prevailed, and one saw 'the Bible, the Cards-the Brutes and the Laws, on one stool – The magistrate sitting in his Chair, and administering Oaths-many in the Crowd, at the instant Cursing and Swearing-While others intoxicated with Liquor, were calling for 'tother ½ Pint.' On Saturdays militia officers held their musters, merchants held their auctions, and planters met to bargain and trade. Shooting matches, dancing, drinking and reveling occurred. These colorful assemblies, 'carried on under Eye of the Magistrates....even by them,' attracted more people than did church the next day."

"The formal institutions-militia companies, justices of the peace, dissenting churches-moderated the disorder of the Back Country life, but these institutions were themselves subject to the eroding effect of Back Country turbulence. Hence their role in Back Country society was ambiguous. The justice of the peace, for example, was a man of prestige and influence, yet his sittings were often marked by unseemly behavior in an atmosphere of levity and tumult."

Over the next several years, the lawlessness in the backcountry became rampant. Rape, murder and torture of farmers and merchants rose to an alarming level. Those that were captured and sent to Charleston for trial were often pardoned by the royal governor. Frustration began to grow and eventually led to the creation of a group of vigilantes who came to be known as the Regulators. Justices of the peace were threatened not to have the criminals arrested and these justices were themselves the victims of the lawless and flagrant outbreaks of violence. Thus, many of these men charged with efforts to enforce the peace joined the Regulator movement to actually bring peace and order to the region.

Law and Order Comes to the Backcountry: The Story of the Regulators.

The Cherokee War of 1760-61 and the continued lawlessness of the back country led the prominent merchants and farmers of the region to continue to demand the establishment of courts in the region. These demands did not fall on deaf ears. The House of Commons petitioned the royal government in England to provide these stabilizing institutions. However, several factors caused the crown to oppose the creation of courts in the interior.

A limited authority had been granted to colonial assembly in 1721, to establish Precinct courts. As a result, courts of pleas, assize and jail delivery were established in several counties along the coast. No development of the upstate had begun at this time. Five magistrates were to be appointed by the governor to preside over each of these courts. One judge would be the president. They were to preside four times a year and were given limited civil authority and criminal jurisdiction that did not include cases with penalties of life and limb.

The courts could administer estates, issue licenses for taverns, handle affairs of orphans and administer the distribution of estates when persons died without a will. Citizens could plead their cases in the courts. In 1722, the courts were empowered to build court houses in each county. None were ever built and most people took their business to the Court of Pleas in Charleston. Thus early experiments with courts outside Charles Towne were unsuccessful.

Additionally, since the colony began there was only one provost marshall or high sheriff. He was appointed like most officials as a reward for some service provided to the English government. The provost received a fee for every legal process served and, although he had some assistants, he did not want these fees to be diluted by having local sheriffs in the districts of the colony to receive a portion of the fees. Accordingly, some method had to be devised to compensate the provost for his lost revenue if a system of courts was established in the interior.

A major stumbling block was how to determine the tenure in office for judges. The crown wanted judges to be removed at the pleasure of the king. The colonists wanted the judges to serve "during good behavior." Efforts to establish courts in the back country for years were stifled by these competing interests.

While this battle was going on, violence and lawlessness continued to grow in the interior. Finally, in 1767, a group of prominent men from the back country decided to deal with the problem and bring law and order to the region. This was the beginning of what came to be known as the Regulator Movement. Driven by a desire to protect themselves and their property and a desire to force the colonial government to establish courts and other institutions for the establishment of peace and order in the region, the Regulators began to raid outlaw camps. The captured villains were summarily tried and punished by the vigilante group.

For a period of about two years, the Regulators controlled the back country and provided the only law and order available. Not everyone was happy with the Regulators and many were sued in Charleston for their activities. However, when writs and warrants issued in Charleston and carried by assistants of the Provost Marshal were attempted to be served, the Regulators prevented their service.

The colonial government prompted by the governor worked out an arrangement to compensate the provost so that district sheriffs could be appointed. This removed one obstacle to the creation of courts in the back country. In 1768, an emissary was sent to England to help sell a bill passed by the colonial assembly to establish circuit courts for the interior. By the end of 1768, the colonial assembly dropped its demand that the judges serve during good behavior and the Circuit Court Act of 1768 was passed and approved in England.

The act set up circuit riding judges to hold court twice a year in each of the colony's districts. The circuit court had the same civil jurisdiction as the Court of Charleston and had criminal jurisdiction in all but capital cases (involving life imprisonment or the death penalty). These courts would not be established for several more years until funds could be raised for the establishment of court houses. The Regulator activity gradually tapered off and a couple of year later the governor pardoned all who had participated in the movement.

The creation of these local courts would be delayed further by the Revolutionary War which brought independence to the colonies. However the Regulator movement achieved its primary objectives and even resulted in an increased representation of the back country in the colonial assembly.

A Thirst For Independence

With the Indian unrest was calmed and the Regulators retired, relations between the colonies and Mother England began to strain. New taxes and tariffs were imposed and this angered many especially in the low country where tea had become a staple. In the upcountry, these issues were not as bothersome, since those grizzled pioneers and backwoodsmen had enough to worry about just staying alive. As a result, most people in our region were loyal to England. These Loyalists, as they were known, opposed a war to separate from the crown. Accordingly, when Patriots who wanted the war came into the region, they often clashed with the Loyalists. Even after the Revolutionary War began, many of the battles pitted the new Patriots fighting against British and Loyalist forces.

Gradually, however, more and more people were won over to the cause of independence. Some of the most decisive battles of the war were fought on or near Spartanburg. Two of the most notable were the Battle of Musgrove Mill and the Battle of Cowpens, which historians have determined was the turning point of the war towards an American victory.

After declaring their independence, the original colonies set up a Continental Congress to raise money for the war and to organize the newly declared independent colonies. On March 26, 1776, South Carolina adopted the first constitution for the independent colony. During the early days of the colony, South Carolina adopted the system of courts of England. Among the judicial officers approved were magistrates. The Royal Governor would appoint these magistrates. Because they were then as now summary courts, meaning courts that acted quickly and were not required to keep permanent records, little record exists regarding the magistrates.

The new constitution adopted the court system as it existed but made some additions and limitations. Justices of the peace were authorized to be elected by the Legislature but they "not acting in the magistry, they shall not be entitled to the privileges allowed to them by law". Obviously, the constitution intended that existing judicial positions of magistrates were to continue. In further support of this conclusion, another section of the constitution declared "That the jurisdiction of the court of admiralty be confined to maritime cases." Thus, it appears that the constitution intended to adopt the existing system of courts with some simple modifications. Since circuit courts had been established in the colony in 1769 and there was no reference to these in the constitution, the inference is that these courts were to continue.

In 1778, a new constitution was written and indicated in the preamble that it was to be the permanent constitution replacing the temporary one from 1776. South Carolina was declared a free and independent state. The state was to be divided into districts and counties as soon as legislation could be passed. Again, this constitution established justices of the peace which "not acting in the magistry, they shall not be entitled to the privileges allowed them by law."

Without enumerating them, the constitution provided that all other judicial officers (presumably including magistrates) were to be chosen by ballot jointly of the senate and house of representatives, and, except for judges of the court of chancery, were to be commissioned by the governor. The only other reference to courts was again a provision that the court of admiralty be limited to maritime cases.

Throughout the war, people were at risk as the men went off to fight. Marauding bands of soldiers, Indians, and wild animals as well as disease threatened the communities - especially in the still sparcely populated upcountry. During war the circuit court schedule was hard to maintain. Therefore, justice in the Spartan District was carried out in its former primitive way. By 1781, peace had come to the state but Charleston was still occupied by British troops. Civilian government began to function again by 1785, when Judge Pendleton's "County Court Act" was passed. This divided the Spartan District into an independent smaller district from the former larger district it had been a part of.

The Act established more regular sessions of court to be held in the district. Seven Justices of the Peace were given lifetime appointments. They were to hold court in the district every three months with any three of the seven constituting a quorum to conduct business. While they held trials, these judges became more of a governing body than a court. The first seven justices were Baylis Earle, John Thomas,Jr., Henry White, John Ford, William Wood, Henry Macham Wood, and James Jorden.

In June, 1785, near the present location of Anderson Mill on the North Tyger River, the first session of the court was held . The justices elected a sheriff and coroner. In September of that year, the second meeting was held at the Thomas Williamson plantation. This was at the location where the City of Spartanburg is today. The sheriff was sworn in.

At the December term, James Yancey was the first attorney admitted to practice before the court in Spartanburg. Bailiffs were appointed as were grand and pettit (trial) jurors. Plans were begun for the first courthouse. By 1787, a search committee had selected a site, so the justices ordered the building of a courthouse, gaol (jail) and a pillory, whipping post and stocks in what is now Morgan Square, in the City of Spartanburg. Public whippings and public humiliations were the most common forms of punishment ordered by the court upon conviction of most crimes. Therefore, the jail was not designed for long term occupancy. Punishments were carried out immediately upon pronouncement of sentences as a rule.

However, some punishments were more severe. Property crimes were considered the most serious. Horse theft convictions resulted in public hangings. Other thefts were punished by cutting off one or both ears. Larceny today is divided into pettit larceny and grand larceny with the only difference being the value of the property stolen. This punishment was akin to a magistrate ordering the removal of one ear, while a higher court judge upon conviction of the more serious grand larceny would cause both to be severed.

Branding was also a means of punishment to announce to the world the crime that the convict had committed. Of course, tarring and feathering or dragging behind a wagon were punishments doled out both by formal courts and vigilante mobs. Public whippings were usually carried out at one time. However, if the number of lashes was a lot, they might be done at regular intervals. Also, the severity of the application was often part of the sentence with "a heavy hand" being the most serious. None of these forms of punishment seemed "cruel and unusual" as would later be prohibited by the U.S. Constitution.

The Continental Congress ordered that the first census was to be taken in 1790. The population of the Spartanburg District was reported as 8800 with about one tenth of those being slaves. There were 1204 households counted and only about 200 of them reported owning more than one slave. The village of Spartanburg had about 300 citizens. In 1826, Robert Mills published his book "Statistics of South Carolina". By then the district had doubled in size to 16,989. The slave population had increased four hundred percent to 3308. This was due to the increased acreage being planted in cotton. Finally, the village of Spartanburg had increased to 800 citizens.

Spartanburg District was predominately agricultural all the way up to the Civil War. Iron works did develop in the area at the turn of the nineteenth century and two cotton mills were in operation when Robert Mills wrote his "Statistics" book. There were also many mineral springs in the area which attracted people from far distances to come for the medicimal values of the waters. However, the area grew very slowly. In 1810, Jesse Cleveland, who became a leading citizen of the community, described the Morgan Square area of Spartanburg as still having tree stumps and roots throughout. The town's population was only about one thousand by 1850.

In 1824, the Legislature passed a law that established for the first time a formal court of magistrates. In each district in the state there was created a Magistrate and Freeholders Court. In the next chapter, the function and history of this court is explored.

CHAPTER FOUR

Chapter 4 - The Spartanburg District Magistrates and Freeholders Court

The early colonial legislature in 1690 established a procedure for slaves to be tried before two Justices of the Peace and three freeholders for the offenses or murder, rebellion, or conspiracy. This jurisdiction was increased to include minor offenses in 1712. This procedure eventually led to the creation of special courts which were called the District Magistrates and Freeholders Courts.

As a history major at Wofford College, I do not remember any mention of this court or of the process of trying slaves during this era of our history. However, while researching for this book, I discovered an excellent article written by Professor Phillip Racine of Wofford College entitled "The Spartanburg District Magistrates and Freeholders Court, 1824-1865." This article was published in Vol. 87, No. 4 (Oct. 1986), pp. 197-212 of *The South Carolina Historical Magazine*. The focus of the article is that by examining records of the court, a picture can be seen of slave society at the time. Since the court kept good records of the testimony and the outcome of the trials held, patterns can be determined of behavior.

While magistrates existed in the Spartan District prior to 1824, as mentioned in the previous chapter, few slaves actually populated the area until about this time. Mills "Statistics" showed that the slave population grew from about 800 to around 3300 from the time of establishment of the Spartan District. Records of the proceedings in this court are kept and maintained at the South Carolina Department of History and Archives in Columbia. Professor Racine did an in depth study of these records which yielded some interesting information about this time in our history.

Magistrates were the peacekeepers in Spartanburg District – more so even than the sheriff. The legislature appointed ordinary men not trained in the law to keep this peace during the time between meetings of the circuit court. Magistrates had authority to issue arrest orders, grant bail, administer the vagrancy laws, register wills and marriage licenses, and eventually run the Magistrates and Freeholders courts. In their capacity, the magistrates did try whites, but the focus of the formal court was to try slaves and free blacks.

In a lengthy article on slaves' use of the legal system, "Status without rights: African Americans and the Tangled History of Law and Governance in the Nineteenth Century U.S. South", appearing in *American Historical Review*, Professor Laura F. Edwards of Duke University postulates that the whole purpose of law was to maintain peace – not to protect individual rights. In support of this theory, she notes that magistrates were the busiest officers in the court system. People went to magistrates with their complaints and magistrates heard them where they received them, whether in the fields or being woken from their beds. They then held trials in convenient places such as taverns, country stores, front porches, in their own homes, or under a grove of trees.

Professor Edwards presents a picture of Southern culture at the time, where slaves, free blacks, poor whites and women brought complaints to the magistrate under the guise of keeping public order. If a husband drank too much, if there was a feud over a fence line, or if a bully was terrorizing the neighborhood, these people with no real legal rights could present complaints to the magistrate as his responsibility to maintain the peace. They were not attempting to enforce private rights but rather the public interest in a peaceful community.

The magistrates handled similar matters as church disciplinary hearings such as drunkenness, sexual impropriety, and conflicts within a family or with neighbors. By bringing in the magistrate, the matter was escalated into a legal matter rather than the usual mediated solutions. In reality, the solutions offered by magistrates were similar to the mediated solutions. One of the most common means of settling the dispute was for the magistrate to place the accused under a "peace bond". The bond was secured by another person by pledging property for a specified period of time, thereby making another responsible for the conduct of the accused in the future.

Trials, when held, usually drew a lot of interest. Evidence sometimes was produced in what was known as "common reports". These were simply numerous instances of rumors that the community had come to believe. Accordingly, a woman might be guilty of loose behavior or prostitution because it was widely believed in the community that she was capable of such conduct. True rumors were accepted while false rumors were discouraged. The only difference was the degree that the rumor was believed in the community.

Today such out- of- court statements or rumors would not be admitted in court because of the rules of evidence that prevent "hearsay". Even though these rules are supposed to be relaxed to a certain degree in magistrate courts, what was then admissible upon the theory of common knowledge simply could not be used today. However, in these early days of the nineteenth century, rumors were often spread by slaves. Accordingly, although neither slaves or women could swear an oath, they could get this testimony before a magistrate under this common reports acceptability.

Accordingly, Professor Edwards concludes that slaves learned the legal process because they saw it unfold before their very eyes. Therefore, slaves sometimes used the process to advance themselves by exploiting this concept that the peace was the ultimate goal. By convincing their owner that another slave was disrupting that peace, they could get the case before a magistrate. Manipulating the system thus was a way to obtain privileges or rewards they would not have otherwise gotten.

Returning to the Spartanburg District Magistrate and Freeholders Court, the court consisted of a mixture of three to five freemen or magistrates who served as judge and jury. The Spartanburg District had from two to four magistrates serving during the forty-one year history of the court. Each magistrate conducted his own court, and there were no formal courtrooms. Often, the offense was tried at the location of the offense or on a farm or plantation in the district. Appeals were allowed after 1833, but were seldom pursued due to the time and trouble. Only 541 cases were recorded over the four decades that the court operated. That is about one case per month. This is not surprising considering that at most times, the Spartanburg District's slave population was only about one-half of the state's average. At the height, the average number of slaves owned per household was about eight.

What is most interesting about the formal district court is that all capital offenses were heard by this court. Today the magistrate courts do not come close to such jurisdiction. However, when a complaint was brought, the magistrate, if he found merit, became the prosecutor. A group of eight slave owners was selected by the magistrate, from which the accused slave's owner or the free black's guardian chose the hearing officers. Free blacks were required to have a guardian, although this law was poorly enforced.

Professor Racine reached some conclusions that seemed to surprise him in analyzing the cases brought before this court. First, about twenty percent of the complaints against slaves were dismissed by the magistrates as having no merit. In all, about forty-nine percent of the cases resulted in dismissal or findings of "not guilty". Racine speculates that this might be due to a concern for the loss of property rights if more slaves were convicted and received severe punishment. However, working against this theory, is the professor's findings that forty-five percent of free blacks also had their cases dismissed or findings of "not guilty" delivered by the court. This led to his conclusion –"Given the prejudices of the age, the courts seemed careful in examining the evidence placed before them, and on the whole, they were willing to consider extenuating circumstances. In most cases where the court found the defendant guilty, the evidence seems persuasive."

Even in the decade of the 1850's leading up to the Civil War, when unrest among the slaves grew greater, the pattern did not change. More cases were brought to trial, but the percentage of verdicts of "not guilty' increased so that the overall conviction rate remained about the same. However, cases against free blacks increased due to concerns about their activities. Even so, in the decade of the 1850's, only nineteen cases were brought against free blacks.

During the entire time of the court's existence, the most common form of punishment was whippings. Of the 278 guilty verdicts rendered, the sentence of whipping was applied in all but eight cases. Six of these resulted in the penalty of hanging and two to confinement on bread and water. In analyzing the whipping sentences, Racine relates that almost half of these involved lashes of between fourteen and thirty lashes. Ten percent involved less than thirteen lashes and thirty-five percent ranged between thirty-one and fifty-six lashes.

The professor relates that a black who was convicted most likely would receive between twenty-three and fifty-six lashes. The legal limit for whites convicted was thirty-nine lashes, with an average of twenty. Therefore, it appears that blacks were treated somewhat more severely than whites but the difference in punishment was not dramatic.

In evaluating the types of offenses heard by the court, Professor Racine found that more than half involved theft. Another eleven percent involved assault. The court found the defendant guilty more often in assault cases than in other types of cases. Finally, gambling and drunkenness completed the list of most common crimes heard. However, three convictions of murder, two of burglary, and one of arson resulted in the defendants being hanged. Racine indicates his belief that hangings were done sparingly because of the resulting loss of property by the slave owners.

In 2008, Bruce W. Eelman published a book entitled "Entrepreneurs in the Southern Upcountry: Commercial Culture in Spartanburg, South Carolina". It was published by the University of Georgia Press. The author refers to Professor Racine's research but gives his own insight into the functionality of the Magistrate and Freeholders courts:

"Despite indications of procedural informality, the property concerns of slave owners ensured that the accused slaves were not convicted out of hand. Since most of the jurors were slave owners themselves, they recognized the dilemma of authorizing damage to a person's slave property. If all slaves before the court were found guilty, spiteful individuals could bring a charge against a slave as part of a personal vendetta against a slave owner."

Eelman indicated that the court was not without contemporary critics: " There was at least one upcountry legal reformer who recognized the problems of fairness in the loosely constructed slave courts. Circuit judge and lifelong liberal reformer John Belton O'Neal believed that the Magistrates and Freeholders Courts should work not only to preserve the rights of slave owners but to provide basic procedural fairness to slaves themselves....The judge argued that black trials should take place at a courthouse with a presiding judge, magistrate, and twelve-man jury picked from twenty-four."

The author concluded that these arguments received little support because to do so would cause slaves to have rights that were not recognized and would raise their status from that of property.

By the conclusion of the Civil War and especially by the new constitution imposed by the federal government in 1868 during Reconstruction, the District Magistrates and Freeholders Courts were abolished. Under this constitution, justices of the peace were to be elected. However, by legislative act of 1868, the office of magistrate was reinstated, with judges being appointed by the governor on advice and consent of the senate. Thus no elections were ever held. Throughout the history of the magistrate court in South Carolina magistrates have never been publicly elected. There was a period in which advisory elections were held – the results of which the governor could accept or ignore. The governor and the senators more often than not followed the "advice" of the electorate.

Magistrates continued to exercise a significant role in keeping the peace in their local communities, but the life or death authority would never exist again.

CHAPTER FIVE

Chapter 5 - Dark Days and the Renewal

In the period approaching the Civil War, Spartanburg began to expand and prosper. The most significant event was the beginning of the railroad in 1859 – an event that would later lead to Spartanburg's designation as the "hub city" of the South. Additionally, the City of Spartanburg began tearing down many old building and established many new commercial structures in the 1850's. Old cabins were replaced by spacious larger homes with surrounding gardens.

Higher education began to advance with the chartering of Wofford College in 1851. Following that was the establishment of the Spartanburg Female College. The Reidville Male and Female High Schools were established by the Nazareth Presbyterian Church and became very successful. The forerunner of the South Carolina School for the Deaf and Blind was established in 1849 in the Cedar Springs Community.

A new courthouse was built in 1856. It replaced the smaller twenty year old structure on Morgan Square. The Palmetto House, also on Morgan Square, became the social scene for many events over its forty year history from 1850-1890. More doctors and lawyers established offices in the area. Saturday's market day saw many local farmers bring their produce for sale in the downtown area.

It is unclear how Spartanburg would have developed over the next twenty years since this development came to an almost complete stop with the secession of the the South from the Union in 1861. The

Civil War and the period following known as Reconstruction caused the economic growth of the Spartanburg area to grind to a halt.

The Spartanburg District Magistrates and Freeholders Court continued operation until the end of the War. However, national events changed the landscape of the South. Andrew Johnson became President of the United States with the assassination of Abraham Lincoln five days after General Lee surrendered. Though a Southerner, Johnson was opposed to the secession. He was expected by the Radical Republicans in Congress to penalize the South for this action. Instead, he was sympathetic to the South, refusing to punish the former combatants.

Additionally, Johnson refused to support the extension of civil rights to the former slaves. This all came to a head when he replaced Secretary of War Stanton. This angered the Republicans in Congress and they successfully drafted Articles of Impeachment against the president. Though Johnson survived the impeachment trial by one vote, he was crippled in 1868 for the remainder of his term as president.

Radical Republicans became the majority in Congress. They passed the fourteenth and fifteenth amendments to the Constitution. South Carolina, under threats of reprisals, passed the amendments which extended civil rights and the right to vote to former slaves. Women, even in this climate, were not extended the same privileges, thus, a former female slave was free from bondage but had no right to vote.

Military units occupied the South. A new constitution was drafted in 1868 in South Carolina. By its terms, justices of the peace were to be chosen by popular election. In that same year, the South Carolina General Assembly passed a law that the governor would appoint magistrates with the consent of the senate. Thus ,no popular elections were ever held for the office of magistrate. A procedure was established in the mid twentieth century for advisory elections for magistrates. Even though these were often hotly contested elections the governor was not bound by the outcomes.

I remember Judge Ralph Mitchell being terrified that someone would run against him or that the governor would not honor the results of the election. In my youth, I remember him speaking at the often held stump meetings during the election cycle. This is the only time that judges appeared as candidates for judicial office in Spartanburg. Judge Mitchell was always appointed, and, eventually rose to the office of Master in Equity.

Though Spartanburg was not impacted as much as other parts of the state during the Reconstruction period, the economy did suffer. Also, a period of violence began that continued until the end of Reconstruction in 1877. Many black magistrates were appointed. The Ku Klux Klan began a reign of vigilante activity. In Spartanburg these activities occurred primarily between 1870 and 1872. In one sad episode, Damon L. Fordham in his book True Stories of Black South Carolina (2008) indicates that the New National Era magazine of January 12, 1871, reported that Spartanburg' first black magistrate, Anthony Johnson, was killed by the KKK in the presence of his mother. Johnson had been appointed on October 13, 1869. From the end or Reconstruction, it would be over one hundred years until the next black magistrate would be appointed in Spartanburg.

The Spartanburg Herald, in an article published March 4, 1992, related a controversy that had arisen among Spartanburg County's senators over the appointment of magistrates. Senator Glenn Reese, it was reported had offered for appointment a magistrate to serve the Boiling Springs community. However, the Spartanburg County Council refused to fund the position. This controversy would later be resolved in a lawsuit. However, the paper continued to report that the controversy "overshadowed Sen. Ty Courtney's recommendation of perhaps the first black person in Spartanburg County history to be a magistrate. Courtney, in one of his four recommendations, chose Greer funeral home director Warren H. Sullivan, Jr., 32, to serve as a part-time Greer magistrate. " The article quoted Courtney , "To my knowledge, this would be the first black magistrate in Spartanburg County."

While Courtney's motives were commendable, his history was wrong. Sullivan, however, was the first black magistrate in Spartanburg County since Reconstruction. He served honorably until the demands of his business caused him to choose to give up his judgeship and return to private business fulltime.

On February 23, 2003, the Spartanburg Herald published an article authored by Linda Conley entitled "Truth behind fate of first black trial justice unresolved". The author indicated that Anthony

Johnson or Johnston had indeed been killed while serving as a magistrate. The exact circumstances of his death, however, were in dispute. Two versions had been reported with the first related in the WPA book "A History of Spartanburg County" in 1940. This book reported that rumor indicated that injured husbands and wronged property owners lured Johnson from his home and shot and killed him.

The report mentioned in Fordham's book was related in a newspaper published by abolitionist Frederick Douglass. A band of ruffians shot down Johnson's door and ordered his mother to get a rope to hang her son, it was related in the Douglass article. Finally, it was reported that he was shot in the head by the lawless band. Conley continues in her article, "Since little documentation exists, it is difficult to say which account is accurate. Spartanburg native and historian Damon Fordham believes there is some truth in both accounts. He said it is possible there were some wronged property owners because there was a great deal of corruption during Reconstruction, and it is possible Ku Klux Klan members or those impersonating them murdered Johnson."

Known as a dark time in the South, the Reconstruction Period was dominated by corrupt and greedy people who bought public offices. Carpetbaggers, being Northerners who came south with their possessions in a small bag made of carpet material, and scalawags, being southern whites who sympathized with the Republican legislature, took possession of most of the economic resources of South Carolina.

Professor Lewis P. Jones, one of South Carolina's most respected scholars and historians, wrote a book entitled "South Carolina – A Synoptic History for Laymen" which was published during the Bicentennial of the state in 1976. Dr. Jones wrote that the period of Reconstruction was definitely a period of great corruption. Former slaves who were now free had no direction or training. Therefore, many became vagrants. The promise of the Radical Republicans in Congress for a mule and forty acres to these newly freed people never materialized.

Jones notes that all the carpetbaggers were not bad. Several were notable individuals and attempted to make positive contributions to the state. However, they were swimming in a sea of corruption, surrounded by the overwhelming majority of dishonest politicians who had bought their offices. The state was thus robbed of it's remaining resources and former slaves, in most instances, were in worst economic conditions than before the war.

In Spartanburg the occupying force was a division of the Seventh U.S. Cavalry. General George Custer commanded this force, but had his headquarters in Kentucky. He is not known to have ever visited Spartanburg, but his wife recounted that he hated the assignment. In a book written after Custer's death, she noted his dislike of the duties of breaking up distilleries and suppressing the Klan. This to him was not soldier-like.

In 1873, Custer was ordered to the field to fight Indians in the west. Major Marcus A. Reno had been Custer's primary officer in Spartanburg. On June 24, 1876, Custer arrived at the Little Big Horn River in Montana Territory. Major Reno was to join him on June 26. However, Custer chose to attack what he believed to be a small group of Indians on June 25th. To his surprise, the Indian force was overwhelming and he and his army were slaughtered.

With the election of Wade Hampton as governor in 1876, the Reconstruction period came to an end in South Carolina. Dr. Jones describes the election of 1876 as being fraught with corruption on both sides. More people voted than existed and several people bragged of voting numerous times. Bloodshed and threats kept many voters home. A group of terrorists known as Red Shirts kept many blacks from voting, although 17,600 black voters cast ballots for Hampton.

Both Hampton and the Radical Republican government claimed victory. From 1876 until mid-1877 both attempted to govern. When newly elected President Rutherford B. Hayes withdrew federal troops in 1877, Dr. Jones wrote that the carpetbag government finally collapsed. Hampton began to dismantle the changes made during Reconstruction.

Dr. Lewis Jones describes the period between Reconstruction and 1890 as the "Bourbon Period", named for a French dynasty that was described as "having forgotten nothing or learned nothing." This description as Dr. Jones analyzes described a period of time when Hampton surrounded himself with former confederate Generals in political office. Speeches and celebrations commemorated the antebellum period. Grace and charm as well as good manners dominated the period.

Hampton extended some low level government jobs to blacks, and some efforts were made to offer public education. But as Jones describes, this was a period of austerity in government. The theory was the less government the better. As a result taxes were low but so was the assistance of government to infrastructure, education, and industry. For most of the state, this was a stagnant period.

In Spartanburg, in contrast, after Reconstruction, a boom began. The area became the railroad hub of the South, cotton mills began to pop up and prosper and would dominate the economy for nearly a century, the mineral springs brought people from far distances, and higher education prospered with the establishment of Wofford and Converse College.

Spartanburg's population increased about six hundred percent from 1870 until 1890, according to an article in the *Charleston News and Courier* in 1890. The article praised the city's Opera House as the best in the state for entertainment. The Merchants Hotel (later named Spartan Inn), according to the author of the article was the finest hotel in the state. The rooms were lighted with gas and very well furnished and the food was excellent, as described in the article.

In 1881, the city of Spartanburg was given a charter with a population of 3,253. The Opera House mentioned earlier was erected a year later and was actually the City Hall at the western end of what we know as Morgan Square. In that same year, the widow of Dr. Lionel C. Kennedy deeded land to the city for the erection of the Kennedy Free Library. During this time about seventy-five businesses existed in the city. These included four drugstores, one bank, a bookstore, and two weekly newspapers. The previously mentioned Merchants Hotel was constructed at about the same time.

Magistrate courts now presided over minor offenses committed by both blacks and whites. Punishments were less severe than in the past and a renewed usage of the peace bond was experienced. Since magistrate courts were not courts of record, few notes are found of the proceedings in the courts. It is ironic that the most recorded era of the court's activities was during the period of existence of the Spartanburg District Magistrates and Freeholders Court. However, those that served as magistrates had also changed. All were white males until nearly a century later. However, the persons were not necessarily the landed gentry as in the past. No educational requirements would be established until into the late twentieth century. Accordingly, in Spartanburg, men who were popular in the community and were good problem solvers were most often chosen.

The era beginning in 1890, with the election of "Pitchfork" Ben Tillman as governor, set the stage for policies that would last for about a century in South Carolina. The constitution of 1895 established a framework of government that for the most part remains until the present day.

CHAPTER SIX

Chapter 6 - The Tillman Era and the Early 20th Century

Dr. Lewis P. Jones was the best lecturer and teacher that I ever had. He was instrumental in my choice to be a history major at Wofford College. Jones could describe a historical figure in such vivid terms that it was easy to remember the person and their influence on events in the past. Such was his talent making his classes enjoyable adventures into the past.

In his book on South Carolina history for laymen, Dr. Jones demonstrates that ability to bring characters in history to life. He describes a one-eyed farmer from Edgefield with a high shrill voice who was one of the most colorful politicians in the state's history. Ben "Pitchfork" Tillman first emerged in 1885 as a fiery orator who championed the interest of the small white farmer. For five years, he railed against the elite Bourbons who controlled the state until he took control of the Democratic Party in 1890.

The interesting fact is that his followers were not only farmers. As a matter of fact he developed a coalition that included lawyers, doctors, and businessmen. The ultimate goal was to give voice to those who had been excluded by the Hampton followers who lived and governed mostly in the past. In so doing he was instrumental in getting the state to accept a land grant from the Clemson family that led to the establishment of Clemson College in the upstate. Additionally, he helped establish what is now Winthrop University as a college for women.

His two terms as governor led to much antagonism among the classes and much legislation that Dr. Jones describes as racist. He gave fiery speeches against the blacks who had controlled the state during Reconstruction. Tillman's reforms did open up the state to ideas that helped the lower classes and increased the representation of the upstate in the Legislature. A vocal opponent was N.G. Gonzales, a well known newspaper writer, who founded <u>The State</u> newspaper in 1891 whose goal was to get rid of Tillman.

Tillman served two terms as governor from 1890 until 1894. He then was elected as a U.S. Senator and served until 1918. Tillman's influence helped Spartanburg continue to develop as one of the most thriving counties in the state. This is true even though he got a bill passed to limit the number of hours a person could work in a cotton mill to sixty-six per week.

A major goal of Tillman was to rewrite the state constitution. Both <u>The State</u> newspaper and the <u>Charleston News and Courier</u> were opposed to this fearing Tillman would further entrench his "radical" ideas in the document. However, by 1895, Tillman's followers had forced a constitutional convention. The Constitution of 1895 remains today as the framework of our government.

Article V, Section 1, of the 1895 Constitution provided that the General Assembly could establish inferior courts which did not have jurisdiction over cases involving murder, manslaughter, rape, arson, burglary, bribery, or perjury. Section 20 of this article provided that magistrates would be appointed for each county by the governor with the advice and consent of the senate to serve two year terms. The civil jurisdiction of magistrates was limited to disputes of $100.00 dollars or less. Magistrates had no authority over cases involving the title to real estate.

On the criminal side, magistrates had jurisdiction over offenses that carried a penalty of no greater than thirty days in jail or a $100.00 fine. The magistrate would sit as examining courts to commit, discharge or release on bail people charged with offenses triable in the higher general sessions court. This simply meant the magistrate issued arrest warrants and released people on bond who were charged with offenses to be heard in the higher court. The only exception was magistrates could not set bond for or release people on capital offenses (those that carried a penalty of life imprisonment or the death penalty). Finally, the accused had a right to a trial by a jury of six persons.

With a few modifications such as increases in the fine amounts and the amounts in controversy in civil cases, magistrate courts jurisdiction remains essentially the same today. One major change as mentioned in another chapter, was that there were no qualifications to be a magistrate other than residency in the community where the magistrate served and his requirement to be a registered voter. Accordingly, females were disqualified, as were illiterate blacks and whites, since the constitution set a literacy test to vote. The Nineteenth Amendment to the U.S. Constitution would not be ratified until August 18, 1920, which finally allowed females to vote. As a result, it would be another seventy years before the first female served as magistrate in Spartanburg County.

As the turn of the century approached, the City of Spartanburg began improvements to its streets and roads. Surrounding the city textile mills and their accompanying villages grew from eight to about twenty between 1890 and 1916. These were within about ten miles of the city. Inside the city, the population had grown to 11,395 in the same time period. "Horseless carriages" first appeared on the streets of Spartanburg in 1904. By 1908 the city's leaders boasted of having more paved streets than anywhere else in the region. The main streets were widened, paved, and had concrete sidewalks. Electric lights appeared in the main areas of downtown by 1910.

Spartanburg had a number of magistrates to serve from 1895 into the early twentieth century. Based on records of the South Carolina Department of Archives and History, Spartanburg had magistrates serving throughout the county in different districts. The City of Spartanburg District provided for two magistrates. One very interesting discovery that I made while researching this list was something I never expected. As I scanned the register of magistrates suddenly jumping off the page was the name "R.B. Paslay". In 1905 my grandfather served one term as a magistrate in the City of Spartanburg. This revelation floored me since no one in my family had ever mentioned this.

Later in this book, a sampling of the magistrates who have served over the years will be presented. These profiles of the men and women who have served will demonstrate their contribution to the development of the modern day people's court so many people utilize in our current society.

CHAPTER SEVEN

Chapter 7 - The Selection of Magistrates

The selection of people to serve as magistrates has always presented challenges. In the selection of judges for higher courts, the candidates have a body of work to refer to. The judge's skill can be determined by cases handled by the candidate. If the candidate is a lawyer or prosecutor, cases handled by the person can be reviewed. Fellow lawyers or litigants can, and often do, weigh in on the person's legal skills.

Since most magistrates are not lawyers, this background is not available. How can one determine that a person who was a fantastic service station owner would make a good magistrate? The decisions one makes in business do not translate, necessarily, into good judicial judgment. Even those who were good advocates as lawyers may have a hard time adapting to the neutral position that must be taken as a judge.

In the early days, and even in modern times, the office of magistrate was used to reward a friend or supporter of a senator. "To the victor belong the spoils" was often applied as newly elected senators appointed new magistrates. However, political skills alone did not make a person a good magistrate. Examples abound throughout the history of the magistrate court, that the skills needed to be a good judge were not possessed by all who were appointed.

Some who were appointed learned that this was not the job they thought it would be. Low pay for long hours greeted some, who could not adapt to this role. The challenges of making decisions and making them quickly, as is required of a summary court, were too much for some. One judge that I served with lasted only a month until the pressures were too much for him. Others found that the time to do the job interfered with their fulltime employment. Thus, they gave up the job to devote more time to their fulltime employment.

The Spartanburg Herald reported on January 6, 1920, that John D. Hamer, a popular young lawyer had been appointed to replace J.C. Wrightson as judge of the City of Spartanburg. Wrightson was reported to be returning to his private practice of law. The same newspaper had reported on February 25, 1919, that J.C. Wrightson had been commissioned a magistrate, replacing E.F. Parker. Parker, it was reported, was returning to farm and grainery business.

Some have changed their minds. Thus, in reviewing the history of the court, newspaper articles cite judges who left and came back, some several times. I guess they were just gluttons for punishment. Some learned that the job did not have the glamour they thought it would. Some were more interested in the trappings of the job than the desire to make proper decisions.

During the early days of the charter of the City of Spartanburg, some of the magistrates were appointed to reward them for their service in the Confederate army. Thus, one of the earliest and one of the longest serving was Major A.H. Kirby. His story is related elsewhere in this book. However, by the turn of the century, most of the senators from Spartanburg were lawyers. This trend continued until the turn of the twenty-first century. As a result, most of the magistrates appointed as the City of Spartanburg magistrates were lawyers.

In Spartanburg, the local bar association has always been close knit. Lawyers liked and respected one another and trusted fellow lawyers as their judges. They had the opportunity to observe them in court or to get recommendations from lawyers or judges who had observed their work. Therefore, they felt comfortable with these appointments. Thus, it is not surprising that a young lawyer at the age of twenty-eight was appointed to replace long-serving magistrate A.H. Kirby in January, 1915. Additionally, another young lawyer, Lucius K. Jennings, replaced Robert J. Gantt at the same time.

The Spartanburg Herald in an article dated February 7, 1915, reported, "The appointments for magisterial positions in Spartanburg County were made public last night. Governor Manning has made the appointments on recommendation of the legislative delegation to whom the selection was referred by Senator Carlisle." Thus, the senator asked for help in making these appointments.

Perhaps the reason for this was that Governor Blease had suspended A.H. Kirby in the preceding March, appointing one Harrison Ferguson to take Kirby's place. On January 29, 1915, The Journal and Carolina Spartan newspaper had reported that Harrison Ferguson was quoted as saying he had been promised reappointment as magistrate by Senator Carlisle. He had requested information about charges lodged against him by two men from Spartanburg. The paper reported that Ferguson had journeyed to Columbia to fight for his job.

The February 7, 1915, article in the Herald further reported that all magistrate positions in the county had been filled. However, the number of magistrates had been reduced from 24 to 20 to save money for the county. All of these appointments were made on recommendation of the Spartanburg County legislative delegation through Senator Carlisle to the governor. Ten existing magistrates had been appointed and seven had been replaced in addition to the four deleted districts.

Young Edwin Corry apparently was a good magistrate. However, the young judge died at the age of thirty-one. An article in the Spartanburg Herald on June 13, 1918, reported that a memorial service was held at the courthouse the preceding afternoon. Solicitor J.C. Blackwood read a tribute to the recently deceased young lawyer and judge. Afterwards, Judge Sease, the circuit judge, adjourned court until the next day in honor of the memory of the young jurist. Most likely the challenges of the job did not cause the death of the youngest judge to be appointed at that time. However, in 1973, another young lawyer was appointed at the age of twenty-seven as a judge, thus setting a new record for the youngest appointed judge. Thankfully, he survived longer on the bench than his earlier brethren.

Magistrates continued to be appointed on recommendation of the local senator for many years, with the senators seeking advice from the community for persons to appoint. In the early 1950's, Spartanburg passed a local law to help the senator in his choice of appointees. Candidates for magistrates would have to run in a primary election. Though this election was advisory only, the senators believed that by appointing a person chosen by the people of the community, the choice would be a safe bet.

The elections were apparently hotly contested in many communities, with the local newpaper reporting the election returns. In an article in the <u>Spartanburg Herald</u> on March 24, 1960, it was reported in an interview with W.C. O'Shields, who happily was unopposed for election, that the elections had begun six years earlier. He related that he had been appointed several times by different senators to serve in the Districts of Startex and Tucapau. Throughout the history of the county, by examining the records provided by the Department of Archives and History, it is clear that some judges served in different districts at different times. Some districts were renamed, some eliminated, and sometimes, judges simply moved and found the opportunity to serve as magistrates in a new district. On rare occasions, the senators ignored the results of the advisory election and appointed someone other than the winner of the election. However, the whole purpose of the election process was to take pressure off of the senator for his appointments, thus the election winner was usually appointed.

The unsavory nature of campaigning for a judgeship led to much criticism of the process. Accordingly, the <u>Spartanburg Herald</u> on March 2, 1979, reported that Governor Richard Riley had filed suit against The Spartanburg County Election Commission challenging the legality of the process. Riley alleged that Article V of the State Constitution provided for no election. Additionally, the suit alleged that Article I on the Constitution was also violated by delegating to the people the authority of the governor to appoint magistrates with the advice and consent of the senate.

On March 12th of the same year the paper in an editorial supported the lawsuit. Senator Horace Smith was quoted, " I feel the reason for our county being named is because it has the 'cleanest' and best statute which provides for the election of magistrates." He further stated that the lawsuit was brought to "clear the air as to the question of magistrates participating in elections." On April 10th of the same year, the newspaper reported on proposed legislation to add the City of Spartanburg Magistrate District. Senator Smith had met with the existing magistrates who criticized the law for not providing for the election of the judges of the new district. Smith stated that the election law only applied to magistrates outside the city. He indicated that the city magistrates had not had to be elected.

Shortly thereafter, the Supreme Court struck down the practice of advisory election of magistrates. Thus, once again, the senators were presented with the challenge of selecting magistrates. Advisory committees were recommended to help the senators make the decision. Also, suggestions were made that magistrates should go through a version of the screening that was conducted by a legislative committee that helped clear candidates for higher judgeships. None of these suggestions ever came to fruition.

Unfortunately, a process began to become more popular with the senators in the early 1990's. Seizing on the process that magistrates retained their offices until their successors were appointed and qualified, the senators realized that if they let the judges' commissions expire, they could leave them in office unless they committed some unpardonable act. The senator then would not be blamed for appointing a new judge who did not make the grade. The old tried and true judge, who most frequently had been appointed by a predecessor of the current senator, was a safe bet. If he messed up, the current senator could not be blamed for appointing him, but he could replace him by naming a successor.

The process became more and more acceptable to more senators, until more than one half of the state had judges in this limbo state known as "hold over". In some counties all of the magistrates were held over. The process, however, came under much scrutiny, and newspapers began to editorialize against the process. The State newspaper was the first and most frequent critic of the process. Gradually, more news outlets across the state joined in. However, the Spartanburg Herald began reporting on the issue in an article published on June 19, 1990. Quoting Terry Leverette, of the South Carolina Court Administration, the article reported that ten of Spartanburg's fifteen magistrates were in hold over. The remaining five's commissions were to expire on April 30, 1991.

Finally, on July 5, 2008, an Associated Press report was picked up by most of the newspapers around the state. The Rock Hill Herald reported ," A third of South Carolina's magistrates are in a special 'holdover' status- several going on more than ten years, which, critics say, gives state senators too much control over them". The article continued, "Critics say that gives senators too much influence over the state's 314 magistrates, especially senator-attorneys who practice before the magistrates they nominate." "I don't favor keeping them in holdover status. It leaves a suggestion of pressure on the judiciary.", the article quoted Chief Justice Jean Toal as saying.

The report indicated 107 of 314 magistrates, or 34 percent, were in this status. Spartanburg had the most with 18. More than half the magistrates in holdover had been there for more than two years – four for over ten years. John Crangle of Common Cause said the practice had been going on for "years and years" and "undermined the independence of a magistrate."

On July 10, 2008, the Spartanburg Herald in an editorial criticized the practice, "Some defend the provision of state law allowing holdover status for magistrates. They say they wouldn't have to wait four years to remove a magistrate not doing his job, but this oversight by senators is unnecessary. The Supreme Court could remove a magistrate at any time for mismanaging a courtroom. Many of the state's magistrates are competent jurists of impeccable character and who will tell you they prefer a cleaner system of appointments. Many of the state's senators would prefer to keep this power totally in their hands. South Carolinians should push for a change that restores full faith and credit in the judiciary."

Local officials joined in the call for a change in the process. Seventh Circuit Solicitor Trey Gowdy frequently criticized the procedure. Prior to being elected a senator from Spartanburg, Lee Bright wrote an Op-Ed piece in the Herald expressing his opposition to the abuses described in the hold over of magistrates. Gradually, senators across the state began to appoint their magistrates, and in Spartanburg, most of the magistrates were given the respect of an appointment.

By this time, the law had changed to require candidates for magistrate to pass an aptitude test prior to being offered for appointment. The requirement to be a magistrate now involved appointing only those with a four year college degree. Spartanburg now also had a group of senators who had pledged to work together for the good of the county. This was refreshing and turned out to benefit the court immensely.

One other event had occurred that changed the selection process for magistrates. Up until the middle of the twentieth century, Spartanburg had only one senator. He was elected in a county wide election. Even after Spartanburg acquired additional senators, these new senators were elected county wide. As a result, the senator appointed magistrates for all the different districts in Spartanburg County. About the middle of the century, the system changed so that senators were elected in districts. As a result, the senators still had the legal authority to appoint all the magistrates in the county. However, they agreed that if a senator wanted to appoint a magistrate in his senate district, the other senators would agree to that appointment. Judges that worked at the courthouse would be by consent of all the senators, but they began rotating the appointments so that each senator would be the primary appointing senator of a particular judge.

In all cases the appointments required unanimous consent of all the senators to be effective. Accordingly, to replace a judge at the end of his term required the vote of all the senators. If one senator objected, the judge would stay in office in holdover. As a consequence, even if the majority of the other senators wished to replace a judge, it could not be done. This was by a long standing senate rule.

A bill was introduced in the beginning of the 2004 senate session that would change the rule. The new rule would allow a "super majority" of the senate delegation of a county to make the appointments. As defined, the population of a senator's district determined his percentage of the potential super majority. To make the appointment, two or more senators might be necessary to form the super majority. As a result, in a few instances, the super majority did make changes to the magistrates who were appointed. Fortunately, in most instances, the senators were able to come together unanimously for their future appointments.

Thus, the selection of magistrates has gone through a series of changes. Upon enactment of the Judicial Reform Amendment, all judges were required to retire at the age of seventy-two. Prior to that several judges continued to serve into their eighties. New educational requirements have meant today's pool of potential judges is better educated than ever before. Judges who are not active attorneys were required to take and pass a certification examination within one year of taking office and every seven years thereafter. Continuing education requirements were also required of magistrates. As a result of all this, todays magistrates are well prepared to meet the daily challenges of their jobs.

CHAPTER EIGHT

Chapter - The Battle Over Magistrate Appointments

The issue of who appoints magistrates should be easily determined. From the very first constitution of the state until the current 1895 constitution in force today, the governor appoints with "advice and consent of the senate". The senators "advise" by sending nominations to the governor and they "consent" by confirming the appointment when the governor sends the nomination back to the senate.

In the 1912 case involving Spartanburg County magistrates, State ex rel Lyon, the governor was determined by the supreme court not to have the authority to choose a magistrate that the senate had not agreed to. The senate had the last word, even in cases where the governor thought the magistrate was not suited for service. On several occasions, the body overrode the governor when he had suspended a Spartanburg magistrate.

Apparently, however, it became a custom for the senator to confer with his local members of the House of Representatives when making these appointments. On February 8, 1913, six members of the House from Spartanburg sent a letter to Governor Cole Blease which read: " Dear Sir. We the undersigned, members of the Spartanburg delegation in the General Assembly, have been entirely ignored in the matter of recommendations of Magistrates for the county of Spartanburg by Senator Carlisle. It is our understanding that it has always been the custom of the Senator and Representatives to meet and agree upon the recommendations, the majority controlling. In this instance Senator Carlisle has absolutely ignored us, thereby treating us with discourtesy; and, representing a large majority of the citizenship of Spartanburg county, as expressed in the recent primary election, we respectfully recommend the following for appointment as Magistrates, and ask that your Excellency do appoint them, regardless of whatever recommendations may be made by Senator Carlisle:" Then followed a list of twenty names for appointment.

On February 10, 1913, the governor had the letter read into the record of the Senate and concluded, "I respectfully request you to confirm these appointments, and thereby probably save much unpleasantness and ill-will." The senate then went into executive session. After returning to the regular session, the senate confirmed eleven of the twenty names submitted by the House members through the governor.

What had apparently happened is something that has happened throughout the history of the appointment process. The senator had decided to reduce the number of magistrates in the county to save money for the county. Apparently, after this dispute, Senator Carlisle and the local House members came back together since the Spartanburg Herald reported on January 6, 1915, "The appointments for magisterial positions in Spartanburg county were made public last night. Governor Manning has made the appointments on recommendation of the legislative delegation to whom the selection was referred by Senator Carlisle." The newspaper reported on February 7, 1915, the list of the appointed magistrates and noted that the number had been reduced from 24 to 20 to save the county money.

The Spartanburg Herald reported on February 18, 1933, that a recently passed law called the Burnett Magistrate Bill, purported to abolish some magistrate positions. The Spartanburg County attorneys had written an opinion that concluded that the office of magistrate is a constitutional office and could not be abolished by the General Assembly. "In their opinion, written by Mr. Sutton, the attorneys held that magistrates now serving and where no successor is designated in the act, shall continue to serve until their commissions expire and their successors are appointed and have qualified. The opinion holds that magistrates for whom the act designates successors shall accept the following salary 'cuts': Spartanburg Nos 1 and 2, $1500 to $1200 a month, Chesnee $350 to $250 a month, Inman $500 to $350, Enoree $250 to $150, Landrum $150 to remain at $150, Lyman $400 to $350, and Woodruff $500 to $350."

The attorneys' opinion indicated that where magistrates had no successors appointed, their salaries would remain unchanged. Thus the opinion indicated that a magistrate's salary could not be reduced during his term in office, but the salary could be reduced if another judge succeeded him. Additionally, senators could not remove a magistrate, but could replace one at the end of his appointment term.

On May 5, 1961, the <u>Spartanburg Herald</u> reported on a recurring theme that there were too many magistrates in the county. The paper reported that Senator Charles Moore had introduced a bill in 1955 to reduce the number of magistrates in Spartanburg County from 12 to 7. He changed his mind and settled on 13. These magistrates were to be elected. Convinced that the magistrates were generating not enough revenue, he was reintroducing a bill to reduce the number of magistrates. The paper reported that in 1958 the Spartanburg County grand jury recommended reducing the number from 13 to 7, finding "some magistrates have hardly any duties to perform while others are swamped."

In another chapter, the battle over reinstating the City of Spartanburg Magistrate District, upon ratification of the Judicial Reform Amendment in 1979, is detailed. However, the passage of the amendment set in motion a battle that would continue for many years to come in Spartanburg. The existing magistrates believed, with good reason, that efforts to eliminate their positions would be made.

The first salvo came in an article published in the <u>Spartanburg Herald</u> on February 28, 1980, quoting the results of a recent audit of caseloads by the S.C. Court Administration, the four City Magistrates handled 9,314 cases compared to the total for the other 13 magistrates at 14,789. The paper noted, " The Judicial Reform Amendment, effective last November, called for the discontinuation of the election of magistrates. The county has allowed the magistrates to finish out their terms, which expire at the end of the year."

"The U.S. Supreme Court has already rendered an opinion upholding the Judicial Reform Act in discontinuing the election of magistrates. That leaves only two choices according to law. These call for the local senators or a screening committee of the local legislative delegation to recommend to the governor the reappointment of some or all the magistrates for two-year terms , or establishing a central magistrate court where four or five magistrates would process all misdemeanor cases."

The article indicated further that the local delegation favored the central court concept but no decision had been made yet. Chief Magistrate Roland Jones was quoted as indicating that some realignment in the court was needed, especially considering the caseload figures. However, the magistrates had some political allies, especially in County Councilman Joe Watson and in Representative David O. Hawkins, who had served as magistrate for several years. Accordingly, the magistrate districts survived.

However, the issues were framed. Some believed that magistrates should justify their existence by bringing in sufficient monies while the other side believed that service to the local communities was the most important issue regardless of the amount of monies collected. Adding fuel to the fire was the move to create central traffic courts in every county. A federal grant had been obtained by the S.C. Court Administration to set up pilot programs in seven counties including Spartanburg. Edward Atwater, the Director of Court Administration, held a meeting with officials from the seven counties on December 19, 1979.

In an article in the Spartanburg Herald on April 8, 1980, the paper reported "There is inherent resistance from magistrates who fear that they might lose their jobs or their pay might be reduced. Atwater explains that it is not the intent of the central court to reduce the number of magistrates, 'but this might be a by-product." The final result was that the county council decided not to establish the court at that time.

For most of the decade of the 1980's , Edward Overcash as chief magistrate was caught in a squeeze over this issue. He, along with the majority of the senators, supported the central court concept. It made sense economically, but many argued that it would inconvenience the citizens. There was also a school of thought that it should not be set up at the courthouse because there was not adequate space. Eventually, in the early 1990's the court was finally established.

By this time, both members of the House of Representatives and

Senators were elected in single member districts. Many wanted their districts to keep their local magistrates as a service to their constituents. Finally, the district magistrates got their champion with the election of Senator Glenn Reese of Boiling Springs. He wanted to expand the number of regional magistrates, not shrink them.

On March 4, 1992, the Spartanburg Herald reported, "State Sen. Glenn Reese of Inman wants a magistrate in Boiling Springs, and he doesn't care if Spartanburg County Council will pay for the judge or not. Reese, disturbed by what he sees as an attempt to unnecessarily consolidate services in the county courthouse in downtown Spartanburg, recommended attorney Frank Adams for the post of part-time Boiling Springs magistrate."

The article continued, "For at least a year he has been fighting for additional magistrates in the county, despite a move towards consolidation. But there is a catch. The county funds magistrates, and this year's budget doesn't include money for a magistrate in Boiling Springs." "The issue of appointing an unpaid magistrate is unresolved", said George Markert, assistant director of S.C. Court Administration. 'It may have to be resolved in the courts', Markert said."

This battle would continue for nearly a decade with Adams attending all the required training for an active magistrate though he had to pay his own expenses. Eventually, as will be seen later, the issue was resolved in the courts. However, this conflict illustrated clearly the county council's efforts to reduce costs versus the argument that provision of judicial services outweighed that effort. Overcash, as chief, came under constant criticism and pressure from the district judges and from Senator Reese.

Some of the district magistrates were very vocal in their criticism of Overcash. Article after article in the local press recounted the battle and Overcash circled the wagons, but little by little, his support eroded. Finally, the Spartanburg Herald reported on December 18, 1992, that Karen Kanes would replace Overcash as chief. Chief Justice Harwell was quoted, "I thought I'd make her chief magistrate for administrative purposes and see if things would settle down."

"It all went back to the district magistrates who got disenchanted with him," said State Sen. John Russell. "There was a lot of ill will at that." Showing how far Overcash's support had diminished, the article went on, "Magistrate Georgia Anderson, who works in the Spartanburg office, said she's not surprised by the change. She advocated a better sense of cooperation now that the change had been made." "Basically, I've been interested in a change," she said."That's been my feeling on it."

For several more years, the battle continued, with County Administrator Roland Windham and County Council Chairman David Dennis becoming more and more antagonistic towards the magistrate court. They refused repeatedly to fund Adam's magisterial position. This became more and more the norm throughout the state, with county governments relying on a statute that said that the county government would advise the senators of the number of magistrate positions available in the county. By this time, however, the General Assembly had passed a law that set an objective standard for determining the number of magistrates for each county. The law provided that there must be one magistrate for every 28,000 people in the county or one for every 150 square miles, whichever was higher. The one magistrate could be divided into four part-time magistrates if desired.

The issue came to a head in 1996 when the State Supreme Court ruled on a case arising in our adjoining county of Greenville. The county council there had decided not to fund several magistrates for economic reasons. The magistrates sued and the court ruled on January 8, 1996 in the case of Sara Davis v. County of Greenville reported in the South Carolina Reporter in Volume 322 at page 73.

The court ruled that the structure for the administration of the state's judicial system was not within the power of local governments to determine. "Accordingly, it is clear that under article VIII (of the state constitution) that counties have no authority to alter the structure of the magisterial branch of the judicial system.", ruled the court. The court further concluded that if the local government could eliminate one magistrate position it might eliminate them all thus " a construction of the statutes which would permit it to abolish a branch of the judicial system would be unconstitutional."

The court made it clear that "counties are without authority to determine the number of magistrates they wish to have." The maximum number of magistrates established by the formula of 1 magistrate for every 28,000 people or one for every 150 square miles must be in place, ruled the court.

It would seem that this would settle the issue. However, the Spartanburg County Council continued to refuse to fund Frank Adams until he filed suit in the year 2000. An article in the Spartanburg Herald-Journal on August 2, 2000, bore the headline "County Officials acknowledge law...Magistrate Judge gets his paycheck". The article began, "Most citizens probably would yawn at the news that Spartanburg County is funding part-time Magistrate Judge Frank Adams' position this fiscal year."

"But County Council's decision to pay Adams not only removes from Spartanburg County the distinction of having the only magistrate in the state that wasn't being paid – it implicitly acknowledges that elected and appointed officials who refused to pay him in the 1990s were breaking the law."

"State Sen. Glenn Reese nominated Adams, a Boiling Springs civil litigation attorney, for his judgeship in 1992, and Gov. Carroll Campbell approved it. But that was contrary to then county Administrator Roland Windham's plan to save money by centralizing Magistrate Court and not funding judgeships in outlying areas. '(Reese) has put the council in a very awkard position,' Windham said at the time."

"On Windham's recommendation, County Council did not fund Adams' position. Neither was the position funded in subsequent years."

The article went on to recount the Sara Davis decision by the supreme court. The assistant county attorney was quoted as not being aware of the decision. Windham, who had moved on to Charleston was interviewed and he could not remember if he knew of the supreme court decision or not, but he was still defiant, "Windham said he still believes the Legislature shouldn't be able to dictate how county officials spend their money."

Adams and the county settled his lawsuit and he continues today to serve the Boiling Springs Community as magistrate. It is clear that without the strong support of Senator Reese, that most, if not all of the regional offices would have been closed. Today, the central court judges and the regional magistrates have a mutual respect for the services provided by their counterparts. The citizens of

Spartanburg County are the winners, being served by what I and many others believe is the best magistrate court in the state.

What is never written about in discussing the philosophical differences in the role of magistrates, is the fact that the court is a court of law. Accordingly, its primary role is to provide justice. The collection of fines and fees is a spinoff of this but is not its primary role. Were the primary role to be the collection of money, then this would have a very chilling effect on justice. People entering the court would believe, and rightfully so, that their fate was predetermined. There would be no public confidence in the fairness of the court.

Since the role of the court is to provide justice for the citizens, the magistrate court should not be judged by the money it takes in. A better test is the money it saves the county. There is no effective way to measure this, but an example might help to illustrate it. A person gets in a fight with his neighbor in the extreme northern end of the county. The local magistrate office is about two miles away, so he drives there and has a conference with the local magistrate. The magistrate, who goes to church with both feuding parties, calls up the other party and tells him the neighbor is there and asks if he can come down to the office.

Upon arrival , both parties have their say and the magistrate listens intently. At the conclusion, the magistrate points out how he thinks each is right and each is wrong. They think it over, shake hands, and leave as friends again. Problem avoided, cost to the county –nothing. This seems like an episode of the old <u>Andy Griffith</u> television show. But this is what goes on in the local magistrate office thousands of times per year.

The scenario if the local magistrate did not exist is that the offended party travels to the central court and explains his problem to a judge who is professional but a stranger to him. The judges finds "probable cause" for an arrest warrant. The magistrate's clerk types the warrant, it is delivered to the sheriff where another clerk enters it into a computer and then gives it to a sheriff's deputy for service. The deputy drives twenty miles round trip to arrest and deliver the accused to the County Detention Facility. At the jail a clerk fingerprints and photographs the accused. He then awaits a judge and is fed a meal while waiting.

When the judge sees him, he agrees to release him on bond. A magistrate's clerk then prepares the bond, a jailer gets the person his property back and he is released from jail. Two days later, the neighbor is no longer mad, so he goes to the court and dismisses his warrant. Benefit to the county –zero dollars, cost to the county – many dollars. Every individual who had contact with the warrant or the accused cost the county money. Multiply that by the many disputes settled by the local magistrates and the savings to the county are great – but they do not show up on a bottom line.

The interesting thing about this whole issue is that the magistrate court as a whole is one of the few revenue generating agencies of county government. Virtually all the fines and fees collected go to the county, whereas fines and fees collected in the circuit courts go to the state treasury. The magistrate court generates several times its cost of operation in income. This money is instrumental in balancing the county budget annually. Therefore, even if one magistrate district is not generating its cost of operation, the overall system makes up the shortfall.

Unfortunately, the desire of county government in Spartanburg County and other counties is still to control the number and location of magistrates. Citizens should insist that this never happens because it would cause them danger of not having help in time of legal troubles.

CHAPTER NINE

Chapter 9 - The City of Spartanburg Magistrates

As described earlier, the City of Spartanburg in the early twentieth century was a bustling community. With all the activities going on in the community, certainly crime was likely to occur. Therefore, the need for magistrates to deal with this led to the appointment of two judges designated for the City of Spartanburg Magistrate District. From its early beginnings, those appointed tended to be lawyers. Even though there were no educational requirements to be a magistrate, apparently the local senators and the governor concluded that an area like the City of Spartanburg would best be served by judges with legal training.

A few examples of early judges of this district are as follows:

Maj. A.H. Kirby

A.H. Kirby

    Born near Pacolet Mills on January 1, 1829, Augustus Hillard Kirby, helped farm his father's land until moving to Spartanburg at age eight. He later worked with his brother in the mercantile business . At the beginning of the Civil War, he enlisted , but was not physically able to fight in combat. He was assigned as the Quartermaster for the Confederacy stationed in Spartanburg. The quartermaster corps of an army is the supply office – like the general store for an army. He rose to the rank of major .

    Kirby became very active in establishing the Methodist religion in the area. He was such a staunch Methodist and so instrumental in promoting the denomination, that he became known as "the Patriarch of Spartanburg Methodism". After Reconstruction, he was elected as chairman of the Spartanburg County Board of Commissioners.

    In 1890, Major Kirby was appointed a City of Spartanburg Magistrate. He would serve in that position until 1914. However, an event occurred in 1911 that would set a precedent for future appointments of magistrates. After the legislature had adjourned in 1911, Governor Cole Blease suspended Magistrates A.H. Kirby, D.T. Gossett, E. Potter, and W.C. Harrison. In their places , he appointed, without the advice and consent of the senate, J.M. Bowden, S.S. Tiner, W.R. Tanner, and T.O. Fowler. In 1912, when the senate reconvened, the senate refused to confirm the new appointments.

The Attorney General then instituted an action before the State Supreme Court to determine "the tenure by which a magistrate holds office under the Constitution and statutes of this state". The title of the action was <u>State ex rel. Lyon, Atty. Gen, T. Bowden et al</u>. It is reported in volume 92 of the South Carolina Reports beginning at page 393. In this case, the Supreme Court ruled that the governor had no inherent power of appointment. His power to appoint must be derived from the constitution or from statutes passed by the legislature. The court found that the Constitution of 1895 provided that magistrates were to be appointed by the governor for a period of two years "and until their successors should be appointed and confirmed." These appointments were to be made with the advice and consent of the senate.

"From these considerations the conclusion is inevitable that there were no vacancies when the Governor attempted to appoint without the advice and consent of the senate, that the appointments were without authority of law, and were of no effect. The term of office of Kirby, Gossett, and Potter extended from their appointment, with the advice and consent of the Senate, in February, 1909, for two years and until their successors should be appointed by the Governor, by and with the consent of the Senate, and should qualify. The Constitution and statute law of the state provide that the Governor should appoint their successors and submit the appointment to the Senate for its consent at the expiration of two years from February, 1909,; that is, a the session of the Senate in 1911 and the session of 1912. It is thus evident that there has been no appointment of successors to these magistrates by and with the advice and consent of the Senate; that their terms of office had not expired and the offices were not vacant when the Governor undertook to appoint without the advice and consent of the Senate and during a recess, Bowden, Tiner, and Tanner as magistrates; that these last appointments were of no effect; and that Kirby, Gossett, and Potter are still lawful magistrates of Spartanburg county.", ruled the court.

Major A.H. Kirby then was returned to his office as magistrate and served until January 6, 1915, when Edwin E .Cory was appointed by governor Manning with the advice and consent of Senator Carlisle and the Spartanburg legislative delegation. At the time, Kirby was eighty-six years old and had served as magistrate for twenty-four years. His health was failing and he died on June 8, 1917, after a long illness. The Spartanburg Journal and Carolina Spartan _newspaper did a front page story on the judge's death which included a picture of the long serving magistrate. He looked the part of a Civil War officer with his long grey beard.

The article praised Kirby with its comment "As a magistrate he was sympathetic to unfortunate people in the clutches of the law, he seemed to know human nature as few people knew it, and many instances in which he acted as peacemaker between husband and wife, neighbor and neighbor, may be found in the records of the office of trial justice".

In the same newspaper , in an article published on January 9, 1915, at page 8, the writer recounted a case tried before Magistrate Kirby. The article noted Kirby's history as a staunch Methodist as he presided over a trial of a man accused of selling liquor. The prosecutor asked the defendant if he had not once been a Baptist preacher. The defense lawyer objected to the question as not being relevant. After stroking his long beard, Judge Kirby remarked, "Objection sustained. I've often heard the circuit judges rule that you can't ask a man a question that tends to disgrace him!"

In addition to his other contributions, Kirby was a local historian. He had attended the funeral of a local Revolutionary War hero James Seay in 1850. He was therefore asked by the Daughters of the American Revolution to give an address at the placing of a marker commemorating the service of the hero at the church graveyard of St. Timothy's Chapel near Arkwright. He wrote the address, but due to illness, could not attend the ceremony.

On a blog called "Hub City Historian" dated July 17, 2008, it was written that most of the land currently comprising the Hampton Heights community in the mid nineteenth century was owned by Major A.H. Kirby. Kirby's home sat at the top of a hill where Bethel Methodist Church is located which was referred to as Kirby Hill. This area became the encampment grounds for the Union army during its occupation in the days of Reconstruction.

Accordingly, Kirby became one of Spartanburg's most

influential citizens and one of the earliest and most colorful of the magistrates of the City of Spartanburg Magistrate Court.

Robert B. Paslay, Sr.

In 1905, Robert B. Paslay, Sr. was a lawyer who had settled in Spartanburg after graduating from the University of South Carolina School of Law in 1902. He was one of five in his graduating class and was welcomed into the legal community by established lawyers like Leland Bomar. Robert Paslay's name was often misspelled as Pasley and sometimes even Paisley. Some of these misspelling are as a result of a long family history of various spellings of the name. Also, the Paslay family descended from ancestors who lived in Paisley Scotland.

This arm of the Paslay family was from Laurens County, where Robert was born in 1876 in the town of Mountville. He grew up in the old Paslay home which was a log cabin structure and the oldest house in Laurens County. Upon arriving in Spartanburg, Paslay became very active in local affairs. In addition to being a magistrate, he became the first City Recorder for Spartanburg.

Serving as a City Magistrate from 1905-1907, Paslay then served in the state legislature and, in 1910, he was appointed as one of two members of the Spartanburg County School Board. He was a presidential elector who cast his vote for Woodrow Wilson for President of the United States. He served as president of the Municipal Democratic Election Board. During World War II, he served on the Selective Service Appeal Board.

During Paslay's legal career he became friends with James F. Byrnes, who served as Secretary of State of the United States, Justice of the U.S. Supreme Court, and Governor of the state. Robert Paslay, Sr. argued several cases before the South Carolina Supreme Court. At age 84 when he died, he was the oldest member of the Spartanburg County Bar Association.

My grandfather was nearly seventy when I was born, and I was only fifteen years old when he passed away after a long illness. As a result, I did not spend a great deal of time with him. He was an active lawyer with a fairly heavy case load and spent very little leisure time. Elder members of the Spartanburg Bar have told me stories of trying cases with him. Apparently he had the habit of jingling his keys in his pocket as he examined witnesses.

One attorney told of first meeting my grandfather. He went to the magistrate's office, which was in the stately courthouse that was in use from 1890-1958. The office was on a lower floor and the courtroom was very small. Therefore, he was waiting on a bench in the hallway to see the magistrate. At that time, magistrates issued warrants for husbands who failed to support their dependents. These non-support warrants were very common until the domestic relations court (later Family Court) was created in Spartanburg. My grandfather approached the young lawyer shaking his finger at him and said "Why haven't you supported your wife!" After the episode, they became friends, but, apparently, the first encounter was memorable.

Robert Joseph Gantt

The Federal Writer's Project published a series of biographies from 1936-1940. D.A. Russell interviewed and wrote such a biography on February 15, 1939, on Robert Joseph Gantt. The author writes that Gantt served as a city magistrate from 1905 until 1917. However, the registry of magistrates for Spartanburg provided by the South Carolina Department of Archives and History shows that Judge Gantt was first appointed on February 27, 1911 and again on February 8, 1913. Since he does not appear again, we can assume he served two terms from 1911 until 1915.

Judge Gantt was born in 1872 in Georgia. His father was a very influential newspaper editor in that state. In 1891, he moved his family to Spartanburg to establish a newspaper called the Piedmont Headlight. Gantt's father became a staunch supporter of Ben Tillman, and became influential in South Carolina politics.

Robert Gantt graduated from the University of Georgia before coming to Spartanburg with his father. He obtained a position in the Department of the Interior, then as secretary to Senator Irby. He studied law at night at Georgetown University. After graduating nineteenth in a class of two hundred, Gantt returned to Spartanburg to begin a forty-six year career in the practice of law. Then he served as a city magistrate and later a United States Commissioner for ten years.

In his youth, Gantt had met Jefferson Davis, former President of the Confederacy, when Davis came to visit his father in Georgia. Gantt's grandfather served as a Major in the Confederate army. Gantt later married Dr. L. Rosa Hirschman of Charleston. The author notes that Mrs. Gantt "was a remarkable woman in view of the fact that women doctors were not looked upon so favorably in a town the size of Spartanburg."

The author quotes Judge Gantt as saying , " In my years service as a magistrate, and in observing cases that have come before others, I have noted that a magistrate is pretty close to humanity, so to speak. He is called upon to make decisions in all manner of cases". As an example, the judge told the writer the story that was related to him by a young deputy sheriff who often visited the judge.

Several years before Judge Gantt took the bench, a young white girl had given birth to a child out of wedlock. She pleaded with an old black woman to take in the baby. Even though the woman had several children of her own, she took in the white baby and raised it as her own. Neighbors began to gossip and summoned the police to investigate. The matter was brought before the local magistrate.

Gant continued, " The magistrate in question, who served years before I did, could find no law covering the case. It was before the days of the juvenile court act, but it was decided that something must be done. So my friend was deputized to go out and see if he could persuade the Negro woman to turn the child over to him. When approached, the Negro woman became hysterical. She declared it was her child, that she had nursed it, reared it and loved the child, and she would not give it up because she held it in trust. She flatly refused to reveal the parentage or the history of the infant. She sent for her husband and he declared that they could only take the child out of the house over his dead body."

"After making his report to the magistrate, and a conference with the people in the neighborhood was held, the magistrate decided that the court owed a duty to the State to see that this white child was not reared as a Negro. Then the magistrate issued an order to the deputy to seize the child. The constable declared that while he questioned the right of the magistrate to issue such an order, he felt it was his duty to carry it out."

The deputy further related that he had to confront the woman's husband who approached him with a pitchfork when he went to get the baby. Drawing his gun, the deputy convinced the husband to give up the child. He further related to Judge Gantt the anguish of taking the child from those that had cared for it and their terrified reaction. This was one of the hardest assignments the deputy ever had.

What the story illustrates is the broad range of authority exercised by magistrates at that time. They served as the conscience of the community. It was their duty to ensure that the mores of the time were adhered to. Keeping the peace and keeping public order were common activities exercised by these judicial officers.

In the period of time from 1895 until 1955 some forty odd persons served as magistrates in the City of Spartanburg District. Some of the notables included J. William Davenport , who later became the Probate Judge, J. Wright Nash, who later served as a county solicitor, and Ralph W. Mitchell, who later became the Master-in-Equity. Most of them did not serve very long. On average each served about six years. One of the longest serving was A.H. Kirby, who served from 1890 until 1914.

The Spartanburg Herald-Journal newspaper in an article dated March 10, 1935, presented recollections by Magistrate W. M. Floyd. Judge Floyd was appointed as a city magistrate on April 15, 1933. Judge Floyd related that since 1885 there had been ten hangings in the Spartanburg County jail and in the livery stable behind city hall. Floyd had witnessed all of the hangings and, in most instances, he had placed the black cap over the head of the doomed man as he made his way to the gallows.

The gallows were erected in the county jail when it was built in 1898. Only two of the hangings were carried out at the jail – the other eight were done behind the city hall. The first hanging was for a convicted murderer who killed the chief of police of Spartanburg and the last had killed a man known as the "Inman Express", since he carried bags between Spartanburg and Inman daily.

Judge Floyd recalled the accused in the first case calling out that he wanted to confess to killing the police chief after the hood had been placed on his head. Floyd asked the reporter who was present to take down the confession. The most memorable of the hangings related by Floyd was the hanging of two black males and one black female on the same day. The two males had been convicted of murder and the female of murder of a baby by poisoning. Floyd related that the female went to her death singing "I'm going to glory Land, Lord".

Floyd's final recollection was the most troubling. A man was hanged for murder in Spartanburg and several years later another man in Georgia, on his deathbed, confessed to the killing. He indicated, he had committed the murder in a local saloon and had placed the gun in the pocket of a drunken man in the saloon. The drunk was arrested, the gun was found, and he was convicted.

The most interesting recollection of Judge Floyd was an incident that occurred behind city hall. The sheriff had a twenty-five foot tall scaffold erected for the hanging. As he was adjusting the cap on the convicted man's head, the sheriff slipped and nearly fell off the high structure. The convicted man reached out and grabbed the sheriff and prevented him from falling – effectively saving the sheriff's life. The sheriff continued with his task to hang the savior. Judge Floyd does not mention if the sheriff thanked the condemned for saving his life before he took his.

A 1948 Spartanburg County Bar Association Photo depicting members at that time depicts the following members who served as magistrates: Robert B. Paslay, Sr., Robert J. Gantt, J.C.Wrightson, John L. Lancaster, Arnold Merchant, J. Wright Nash, J. William Davenport, D.W. Galloway, Esten C. Taylor, Ralph W. Mitchell, Howard Bobo Carlisle and Bobo Burnett. That is 12 out of the 86 members depicted.

In 1955, the General Assembly passed legislation establishing the Spartanburg Civil Courts. Essentially, this simply renamed the City of Spartanburg Magistrate Court, since the judges continued the same criminal jurisdiction as magistrates and had a slightly higher civil jurisdiction. Following the tradition, judges of the court were required to be lawyers. Unlike other magistrate courts, the Civil courts had countywide jurisdiction except for as small area in the lower part of the county. This court continued until 1971, when the General Assembly converted this court into the Spartanburg County Civil and Criminal Court. Over the life of the court the civil jurisdiction had gradually increased to $1500.00 amount in dispute. Like magistrate courts, the court did not have jurisdiction in disputes involving the ownership of land.

Five judges served on the Civil Court. Judge Bobo Burnett and Judge Ralph Mitchell, who were magistrates when the court was formed, served the longest time. They began their tenure on June 27, 1955. Judge Burnett continued on this court until replaced by Thomas J. Dezern on May 4, 1971 at the beginning of the Civil and Criminal

Court. Judge Mitchell became the Master-in-Equity and was replaced by Judge Paul S. McChesney, Jr., on March 25, 1963. Judge McChesney became judge of the Juvenile and Domestic Relations Court on December 28, 1964. He was replaced by George S. Depass on January 8, 1965 who, in turn, was replaced by Ellen Hines Smith on December 30, 1971. Just a few months later the Civil Court was renamed the Civil and Criminal Court.

The criminal jurisdiction of the Civil and Criminal Court (referred to most frequently as the C&C Court) was identical to that of magistrates, but the court had a larger jurisdictional amount in civil cases. This was increased to $2500.00. Again, the court lacked jurisdiction over disputes involving the ownership of land. Judges were required to be lawyers. One of the three judges served as the chief judge of the court and one served as night and week-end judge. This court continued until 1979, when the General Assembly passed the Judicial Reform Amendment, eliminating the non-uniform courts throughout the state. The judges formed the City of Spartanburg Magistrate Court again.

Thomas Dezern was the first chief judge of the court, serving along with Ellen Hines Smith and Wallace Dickerson as the night judge. A couple of years later, on August 30, 1973, Judge Dezern became the County Court Judge and Wallace Dickerson assumed his position. A young lawyer two years out of law school took Dickerson's slot. Later, on April 22, 1975, Charles E. Sanders and Kenneth M. Powell replaced Smith and Dickerson. Finally, in 1978, C. Roland Jones replaced Judge Powell who became a Federal Court Judge. Throughout its eight year history, these were all the judges who served, with the young lawyer serving the longest time.

The local legislative delegation did not want to see the Civil and Criminal Court end. They made efforts to get the Supreme Court to extend its life for a year. These efforts were unsuccessful. Therefore, legislation was introduced to recreate the City of Spartanburg Magistrate District. An article appeared in the April 10, 1979 edition of the <u>Spartanburg Herald</u> describing the proposed legislation. Opposition to the law had developed among the thirteen sitting magistrates, so Senator Horace Smith called them together for a meeting. The recently appointed chief magistrate Manning Edwards expressed criticism that the new magistrates would not have to run in an election as the existing thirteen had. Senator Smith replied that the elections were set up for the rural magistrates and that the City of Spartanburg Magistrates had never had to run.

Smith also related that the elections were advisory only and that the senators could ignore the results and recommend someone other than the winner for appointment. He mentioned that they had done that recently. While Senator Smith was certainly correct that the senators could ignore the results, he was not correct that City magistrates had not had to run in the advisory elections. I remember vividly Judge Ralph Mitchell, before the creation of the Civil Courts, even though unopposed, having to run and fearing that someone else would be appointed.

The biggest opposition expressed by Edwards on behalf of the existing magistrates was the new night duty to be performed by the City District. Most magistrates held their court at night, and being at that time paid by their caseload, they feared a loss of business. "I'm going to tell you this," Senator Smith was quoted by the article as saying, "We need a magistrate in the courthouse 24 hours a day, seven days a week, and that is why I am for this bill."

The final bone of contention expressed by Judge Edwards was that the City District would have a chief judge. The other magistrates feared that this chief judge would be over them. "We only need one chief magistrate", Edwards is quoted as saying. The bill limited the chief judge of the City District to handling administrative affairs of that district only. That judge had no authority over the other magistrates outside the district.

It turned out that Edward's concerns were prophetic. By the end of the year, Roland Jones, who served as chief judge of the city district, replaced Manning Edwards as chief magistrate. From that time forward, every chief magistrate appointed by the chief justice has been a judge from the courthouse district.

The Spartanburg Herald reported On June 28, 1979, that Governor Richard Riley had signed the bill creating the City of Spartanburg Magistrate District that provided for four magistrates. The three existing judges of the C&C Court were appointed and confirmed as magistrates a few days later before the June 30th expiration of the C&C Court. The fourth judge was to be named later.

An article appeared in the Spartanburg Herald-Journal

newspaper dated September 14, 1979 describing the change of the Civil and Criminal Court back to the City of Spartanburg Magistrate Court. By this time, C. Roland Jones had succeeded Charles Sanders as chief judge of the district. Judge Michael Skeen had just been appointed to replace Charles Sanders, who had returned to private practice of law. James Paslay continued as night and weekend judge. A fourth judge had been approved to serve the third shift, and soon, W. Andrew Hughes would assume those tasks. He was appointed on October 4, 1979, and would begin his tasks according to article in the Spartanburg Herald on that day.

"The changeover from the C&C Court to the City Magisterial District has placed more of a burden on the rural magistrates who are issuing more and more arrest warrants and holding more preliminary hearings, Jones says. But the City District still has county-wide jurisdiction which actually increased from the C&C Court because a section around Enoree and Cross Anchor was added to the jurisdiction of the court.", related the writer of the article.

Gradually, the City Magistrate Court became the central hub for the overwhelming majority of the cases. First, with a good bit of opposition, the Central Traffic Court was created where most highway patrol cases would be heard. It is hard to say how much political pressure was brought to bear in opposition to the central traffic court. Judge Manning Edwards, with the support of Sgt. R.T. Pitts of the Highway Patrol expressed concerns that citizens would be inconvenienced by having to come to the courthouse for their traffic cases. Pitts also believed his troopers would have to sit around a long time waiting for their cases to be heard.

The Director of Court Administration, John Patrick, was reported as saying that the pilot project in the state in Richland County was working well. Lt. H.W. Addy, the Highway Patrol officer directing the Richland County troopers was also quoted as being very supportive of the concept. The idea was to rotate in all the magistrates to sit on the court. This was to alleviate the magistrates' concerns that their caseload would diminish and, therefore, their salaries would be reduced.

Finally, Roland Jones, the incoming chief magistrate was quoted as having mixed emotions about the plan. "I am concerned about space, personnel, and judicial manpower." he stated. All of this caused John Patrick to announce that if Spartanburg did not want to participate, he would try other counties. Eventually, by consent of the magistrates, the local highway patrol leaders, and county government, a central traffic court was established. It did not have the official endorsement of court administration and no order creating it was issued by the chief justice.

Then preliminary hearings were centralized as were eventually all jury trials. Again, these were done by common consent and not by official order of the chief justice. Little by little, by common usages, the City District became referred to as the Central Court. Even though no official order of the chief justice created such a centralized court, by agreement among the magistrates and tradition, it was a de facto central court. Finally, on June 24, 2004, Chief Justice Jean Toal issued an official order establishing the courthouse district as an official central court.

Today, in addition to the functions that were centralized, the Central Court operates a Criminal Domestic Violence Court. I am pleased to have put the idea in motion while serving as chief magistrate. County Council voted unanimously to approve the concept, and Chief Justice Toal issued an order approving the special court. All domestic violence cases are heard in this special division of the court. This results in speeding up the disposition of the cases and gives access to the necessary counseling services to those convicted. The solicitor and public defender can focus on one location for trials rather than spread their resources over the entire county.

Finally, a special court called Transfer Court is conducted at the Central Court. This division handles cases transferred by the solicitor, by consent of the defendant, which carry a penalty of no greater than one year. Magistrates handle these matters, thus relieving some congestion in the General Sessions Court. For defendants and their attorneys, as well as victims, the quicker disposition is welcomed.

In this modern world, the Central Court does the heavy lifting, clearing the overwhelming majority of cases brought into magistrates courts. The district judges serving in communities throughout the county are freed up to help assist their citizens on legal matters. Certainly, trials are conducted, but these judges are in a better condition to spend time with people from the community to analyze their problems and concerns. The value of these judges is measured in the counseling and guidance they provide. Cost savings occur every day to local government by the cases the magistrates do not issue by their effective mediation efforts. It is impossible to know how many lives have been saved when an angry person entered the magistrate office and had someone to listen to their complaint and calm them down. These judges truly put the people back in "People's Courts".

City of Spartanburg Magistrates 1895-1955

Name	Appointed	Commissioned
A.H. Kirby	12-31-1894	1-3-1895
J.M. Dean		1-3-1895
G.C. Clark		3-3-1895
J.B. Layton	1-3-1895	
J.L. Shippy	1-3-1895	
J.N. Shields	3-8-1895	
W.G.S. O'Shields		3-3-1896
W.G.S. O'Shields		2-5-1897
J.M. Anderson (resigned 11-17-1897)	3-19-1897 (W.A. Ray appointed)	
U.X. Gunter		8-19-1897
Patillio H. McGowan	3-29-1899	3-1-1899
A.H. Kirby	2-29-1899	3-1-1899
Patillio H. McGowan	2-9-1901	2-14-1901
A.H. Kirby	2-9-1901	2-16-1901
John S. Garris	11-25-1901	12-2-1901
John S. Garris	2-20-1903	2-20-1903
A.H. Kirby	2-20-1903	2-20-1903
A.H. Kirby	2-20-1905	2-24-1905
Robert B. Paslay	2-20-1905	2-24-1905
J.R. Coan	1-18-1907	1-23-1907
A.H. Kirby	3-18-1907	1-25-1907

Spartanburg Peoples' Court

A.H. Kirby (suspended by governor) (3-14-1914)	2-5-1909	2-8-1909
S.M. Wetmore	3-5-1909	2-17-1909
J.M. Bowden	3-20-1911	2-22-1911
Robert J. Gantt	3-27-1911	3-21-1911
C.L. Wyche (vice J.M. Bowden) confirmed by Senate)	6-7-1912	3-11-1912 (not
Robert J. Gantt	2-8-1913	3-12-1913
Harrison Ferguson (vice A.H. Kirby suspended from office)	3-20-1914	3-23-1914
L.K. Jennings	3-8-1915	3-11-1915
Erwin E. Cory	2-8-1915	2-11-1915
J.Y. Cantrell Spbg #2	3-8-1915	2-16-1915
L.K. Jennings	3-20-1917	2-26-1917
Edwin E. Cory	2-20-1917	2-26-1917
J.C. Wrightson (vice E. Corry deceased)	6-7-1918	6-11-1918
E.F. Parker	9-6-1918	9-11-1918
J.C. Wrightson	2-15-1919	2-18-1919
L.K. Jennings	2-15-1919	2-18-1919
John D. Hamer (vice J.C. Wrightson resigned)	1-2-1920	3-6-1920
M.B. Brissie	3-4-1921	3-8-19
L.K. Jennings	3-4-1921	3-10-1921

James B. Paslay

J.M. Hicks	11-4-1922	11-20-1922
M.B. Brissie	3-1-1923	3-12-1923
L.K. Jennings	3-1-1923	3-14-1923
John L. Lancaster	3-24-1925	3-17-1925
M.B. Brissie	2-24-1925	3-18-1925
Arnold Merchant	3-14-1927	3-17-1927
J.D. Hamer	3-14-1927	3-21-1927
J.J. Gentry	1-30-1929	3-1-1929
John L. Lancaster	3-30-1929	3-4-1929
D.T. Gossett	3-29-1930	4-2-1930
Fred D. Ballanger	3-25-1931	3-12-1931
John L. Lancaster	3-25-1931	1-21-1932
A.W. Wells (vice Brissie)	4-15-1933	4-19-1933
W.M. Floyd (vice John Lancaster) 4-15-1933	4-19-1933	
J. Wright Nash (vice A. Wells)	3-3-1935	3-7-1935
D.K. Gaffney (vice W.M. Floyd)	3-14-1935	5-16-1935
Daniel E. Hydrick (vice J.W. Nash)	11-12-1937	11-16-1937
J. William Davenport (vice D.K. Gaffney)		
	5-5-1938	7-1-1938
Daniel E. Hydrick	12-28-1939	3-4-1940
H.M. Carter	2-9-1940	3-14-1940
J. William Davenport	3-27-1940	6-14-1940
John L. Lancaster	3-8-1942	3-14-1942
D.W. Galloway	10-1-1942	10-17-1942

Esten C. Taylor	3-4-1942	2-6-1942
Ralph W. Mitchell	3-25-1944	1-27-1944
B.H. Brockman	3-2-1945	3-7-1945
C.G. Carson	3-2-1945	3-14-1945
Esten C. Taylor	3-8-1949	4-14-1949
Bobo Burnett (vice Esten Taylor)	8-7-1952	8-12-1952
Ralph Mitchell	3-25-1953	5-12-1953

Longest serving:

A.H. Kirby	24 years
L.K. Jennings	10 years
John L. Lancaster	19 years
Ralph Mitchell	19 years
Bobo Burnett	19 years
Edward H. Overcash, Jr.	25 years
James B. Paslay	45 years

Attached are the judges who have served on the renewed City of Spartanburg District

REESTABLISHED CITY OF SPARTANBURG MAGISTRATE DISTRICT

Judge	Appointed	Confirmed
C. Roland Jones, Jr.	3-28-79	6-28-79
Charles Sanders	3-28-79	6-28-79
James B. Paslay	6-28-79	3-28-79
Michael Skeen (vice Charles Sanders)		

James B. Paslay

	10-1-79	10-1-79
William Andrew Hughes 3-24-80	7-3-80	
Edward H. Overcash, Jr. (vice Michael Skeen	)	
	6-9-83	7-11-83
C. Roland Jones, Jr.	6-9-83	11-4-83
Edward H. Overcash, Jr.3-9-83	11-4-83	
James B. Paslay	6-9-83	11-4-83
William Andrew Hughes3-9-83	6-24-83	
Georgia V. Anderson	(vice C. R. Jones, Jr.	)
	9-30-83	9-30-83
Edward H. Overcash, Jr.3-15-87	7-1-87	
William Andrew Hughes5-15-87	7-4-87	
James B. Paslay	5-15-87	7-15-87
Georgia V. Anderson	5-15-87	7-1-87
Joseph T. Petty	6-8-92	6-8-92
Karen L. Kanes	6-10-92	6-10-92
James B. Paslay	6-10-92	6-12-92
William Andrew Hughes3-10-9	26-22-92	
Edward H. Overcash	3-10-92	6-19-92
Georgia V. Anderson	3-10-92	6-19-92
Rubye Calhoun	3-10-93	4-6-93
Robert B. Hall (vice Georgia Anderson)		
	6-6-95	6-19-95
Edward H. Overcash, Jr.3-8-95	3-26-95	

Spartanburg Peoples' Court

Eber C. "Chuck" Gowan, Jr. (vice W.A. Hughes)

| | 6-8-95 | 6-21-95 |

Carolyn B. Waddell vice Rubye Calhoun

| | 3-8-95 | 6-21-95 |

| Joseph T. Petty | 6-8-95 | 6-19-95 |

Larry W. Hutchins transferred to courthouse

| | 6-6-95 | 6-6-95 |

Barry Joe Barnette (vice Joseph Petty)

| | 6-27-96 | 7-10-96 |

Barry Joe Barnette	5-24-99	6-7-99
Eber C. "Chuck" Gowan, Jr. 3-24-99	6-7-99
Robert B. Hall	3-24-99	6-7-99
Edward H. Overcash, Jr. 5-24-99	6-3-99
James B. Paslay	5-24-99	6-3-99
Carolyn B. Waddell	3-24-99	6-20-99
Marcus Kitchens	1-18-2001	1-24-2001

Sarah R. Simmons (vice Carolyn Waddell)

| | 5-14-2001 | 3-11-2001 |

John T. Poole (new judge Jail Division)

| | 6-8-2001 | 6-29-2001 |

F. Douglas Caton (new judge Jail Division)

| | 6-14-2001 | 3-29-2001 |

Nancy C. Atkins (new judge Jail Division)

| | 6-14-2001 | 6-29-2001 |

79

James B. Paslay

James Ashmore (transferred Jail Division)

                                                6-8-2001   6-8-2001

David J. Turner   2-13-2004   2-18-2004

REDESIGNATED CENTRAL COURT JUNE 25, 2004

James Talley (Jail Division) John T. Poole (to courthouse)

                                                2-10-2005   3-22-2005

Jason T. Wall (vice Edward H. Overcash, Jr)

                                              .2-10-2005   3-22-2005

Brian D. Taylor (vice Larry Hutchins)

                                                2-10-2005   3-22-2005

Charles William Jones (vice Johnny Cash)

                                                6-27-2006   7-17-2006

James D. Willingham II   vice John Poole

                                                6-7-2007   3-7-2007

Dwight D. Smith (vice Robert Hall Jail Division)

                                                5-20-2008   3-30-2008

William "Rob" Chumley (vice Brian D. Taylor)

                                                2-15-2009

David R. Turner   4-7-2009   3-17-2009

James E. Talley (Jail Division)

                                                10-29-2009   11-10-2009

James B. Paslay   1-15-2010   1-30-2010

Jason T. Wall   1-15-2010   1-30-2010

David R. Turner   3-1-2011   3-15-2011

Spartanburg Peoples' Court

Dwight D. Smith (Jail Division)

    3-30-2011   4-1-2011

Nancy C. Atkins (Jail Division)

    3-30-2011   4-1-2011

Keith Allen Sherlin vice F.D. Caton (Jail Division)

    5-15-2011   5-30-2011

James B. Paslay   5-30-2011   6-15-2011

Charles W. Jones   5-30-2011   3-15-2011

James D. Willingham II   6-30-2011   7-15-2011

Jason T. Wall   3-30-2011   7-15-2011

Roberto Mark Inclan (new judge)

    6-30-2011   7-15-2011

John Moore (new judge)

    6-3-2011   7-15-2011

Karry Guillory (new judge)

    2-2-2012   2-24-2012

James E. Talley (Jail Division)

    5-2-2012   5-31-2012

Freddie Brown Jr. (Jail Division)

    6-6-2013   6-25-2013

John J. Kessler   6-18-2013   8-16-2013

Quentin M. Wood   3-8-2018   7-9-2018

Daniel Ray Burns (Jail Division)

    4-7-2009   4-22-2009

James B. Paslay

James D. Willingham, II

    3-12-2019   3-2-2019

David James Turner   3-15-2019   3-29-2019

Quentin Michael Wood

    3-15-2019   3-29-2019

Daniel Ray Burns (Jail Division)

    5-21-2019   7-5-2019

Page 58

Jason Thomas Wall

    3-12-2019   3-29-2019

Karry Guillory   5-21-2019   6-3-2019

Keith Sherlin (Jail Division)

    5-21-2019   3-14-2019

John Joseph Kessler   5-21-2019   7-16-2019

Charles W. Jones   5-21-2019   3-6-2019

Jacqueline Moss (Jail Division)

    3-21-2019   3-11-2019

CHAPTER TEN

Chapter 10 - The Creation of the Chief Magistrate

In 1979, a new era began in all the courts of South Carolina. A constitutional amendment was passed called the Judicial Reform Amendment. The law abolished all non-uniform courts, being courts that did not exist in all counties. Therefore, those counties having County Courts lost them. Additionally, Spartanburg and the few other counties who had a Civil and Criminal Court lost these courts also. Many believed that this was a mistake, as these courts took a tremendous caseload from the circuit courts. Nevertheless, this was the law and it must be obeyed.

This resulted in the restoration of the courthouse magistrates. Judges serving on the Civil and Criminal Court were appointed to these positions. As a part of the reorganization under the law, the Office of Court Administration was established. This new agency, under the direction of the Chief Justice, was empowered with establishing administrative rules for the operation of all the courts of the state. An order from the Chief Justice created the position of Chief Magistrate for each county.

The powers given to the Chief Magistrate were enumerated in the order and the order was to be renewed twice a year with the appointment or reappointment of chief magistrates. It is interesting to note that there are chief administrative judges appointed in the circuit court. However, their primary responsibility is to control the court docket. They do not control the other judges' salaries or work schedule.

The chief magistrate, however, was empowered with far more duties and, as a result, the chief magistrate, especially in Spartanburg, became one of the most powerful officers in the county. Magistrates were to meet on a regular basis to be updated on procedures and to arrange a schedule to work at the jail for the issuance of warrants and the release of inmates through a new procedure known as arraignment. This was to be done primarily on weekends and holidays, since we had this covered though the week.

In the last chapter the opposition to the recreation of the City of Spartanburg Magistrate Court was discussed. During the existence of the C&C Court, one of the judges served as chief judge of that court. That judge had no authority over the magistrates serving outside the City of Spartanburg. When the bill to recreate the city district was introduced, it included a provision that one of the judges would be the chief judge of the new district. This raised a red flag with the other magistrates, causing them to believe that the chief judge of the new district would have authority over them.

Prior to the Judicial Reform Amendment, each magistrate did his own thing. There was no formal communications between them. While the C&C judges had some contact with the district magistrates, it was infrequent and casual. These judges liked their independence and resented someone now overseeing their duties. Therefore, there was a strong resistance to the concept of a chief judge – especially a lawyer.

However, the newly appointed chief magistrate had few allies outside the thirteen magistrates with whom he served in the opposition to the creation of the new city district. Judge Manning Edwards, was the only full time district magistrate. He served in the Inman District, and, a couple of months into his term as chief, made public the concern of the magistrates in opposition to the creation of the City of Spartanburg District. Judge Edwards, like all magistrates, was appointed by the governor, but on the advice and consent of the Senate. Accordingly, it was not a wise thing to challenge his appointing senators, all of which supported the creation of the new district.

Fortunately, for Judge Edwards, Senator Horace Smith was used to dealing with controversies. He was one of the state's most respected senators and he approached the job with a calm confidence that helped settle many controversies. He, therefore, called a meeting with the magistrates and listened to their grievances. Then he explained that the chief judge of the new district would have no supervisory authority over the other districts. Senator Smith emphatically stated his support for the new district and the magistrates left the meeting understanding that they needed to be onboard.

The power of the chief magistrate was demonstrated very early in Spartanburg. All of the magistrates were gathered together for their first meeting one evening shortly after the order appointing Judge O. Manning Edwards as chief magistrate. I returned from my supper break to meet all the magistrates, some of which I had never met. Just prior to the meeting, one of the long serving magistrates was organizing an uprising against the new chief magistrate. He insisted he was not going to work at the jail on week-ends and he encouraged all the other judges to refuse also. "What are they going to do to us?" he mused. They all agree to back him up.

After calling the meeting to order, Judge Edwards apologized for having to bring everyone down. He said he was not happy to have to work at the jail, but the chief justice had ordered this and we must all comply. He said there were six shifts that would have to be covered of eight hours each, first, second and third shifts, to begin at 8:00 am, 4:00 pm and midnight. He was going to call the roll in alphabetical order and offer the judges their choices of shifts.

The leader of the mutiny happened to be first. Judge Edwards called him forward and asked him his preference of work shifts. " I am not going to do this!", he declared. Judge Edwards seemed unfazed as he declared, "I am assigning you to work the third shift on Sunday."

As the next judge was called and for each judge thereafter, the judges stated their preference of shifts and never raised a voice of protest. Needless to say, after the meeting, the put down mutineer condemned all his fellow judges, but he worked his assigned shifts for the next several years that he remained a magistrate.

The power of the chief magistrate was established and it has become more and more apparent as later chapters of this story will show. However, in a few short months, Judge Edwards was replaced by Roland Jones, who was the chief judge of the City of Spartanburg Magistrate District. The position of chief judge of the city district was declared vacated by the chief justice, and from that day forward all chief magistrates have come from the courthouse judges.

The magistrates did not warm up to the new position. Resistance came in many subtle ways. The most challenging was the authority of the chief magistrate to set the work hours for the other judges. Even though the judges resisted the jail referral duty initially, it quickly became obvious that one eight hour shift provided them the same income as a week in their office, since most judges were approved for eight hours per week. Therefore, the hours became sought after. The judges began to court the chief or the other judges to assign them more hours. Rivalry thus led to much dissention and dissatisfaction with the chief magistrate. By the time Judge Edward Overcash became the third chief magistrate, much of his term was challenged because of these pressures.

Overcash did many good things for the court, but he was dogged throughout his time as chief by judges who still resented the position's power and authority. Many of these judges had been magistrates for a long time and it was very difficult to adapt to the new supervised system. Judge Overcash served longer than anyone else as chief at ten years. However, there was resentment that the City District had better courtrooms, staffing, and equipment. Overcash made every effort to ensure that the judges had clerks and that their offices were as functional as possible. However, as continues today, budget limitations were difficult for the chief to deal with. While he made every effort to get more for the judges, he was met by resistance from those that paid the bills.

The pressures to perform with difficult odds finally resulted in Overcash being replaced as chief by a dynamic young judge who had joined the court. Karen Kanes became the first, and to date, the only female chief magistrate in Spartanburg County. She took a different approach to the district magistrates. Karen was warm, friendly and very accommodating. She worked hard to get the judges extra hours and better offices. Her first order of business was to invite everyone to her house for a giant Halloween party. Karen demonstrated throughout her time as chief her marvelous people skills and her intuitive grasp of politics.

Karen confided in me later that she had agreed to remain on the court only long enough to repair the relations between the judges. She did not know when she came onboard that she would develop such friendships. She did not want to leave, but her agreed time had ended. Therefore, she left the court to develop a successful career in business and politics. However, her legacy remained, and to this day, all the magistrates that served with her remember her with respect and fondness.

After Karen came Joseph Petty, then Robert Hall. Both had rocky terms as chief because neither had the charm of Karen Kanes. Also, many of the same issues that dogged Overcash recurred, with judges battling over the extra hours and pressuring the chief to increase their office hours. In an effort to appease the district judges, these chiefs alienated the courthouse judges. No chief magistrate could provide everything being demanded since he did not control the purse strings of the county.

The challenge of all persons serving as chief has been to determine exactly what the role of the chief was. On paper, there are certain defined duties as set out in the order of the chief justice appointing chief magistrates. In practice, it is hard to carry out these responsibilities. As all chief magistrates have learned, court administration, county government, the local senators, and the judges serving as magistrates all seem to have different expectations from the chief.

Some judges have expected the chief to provide them benefits that either would be unfair to others or could not be done because of budget limitations. Senators expect the chief magistrate, who is given no disciplinary authority over the other judges, to insure that all the judges act appropriately and not end up being criticized in the press. However, the Canons of conduct for judges, require judges to make decisions that might be unpopular and establish a degree of judicial independence.

What all chief judges come to know, if they did not know it when they began their term, is that cooperation among the judges is critical to the longevity of the chief's term. All of the chief judges, save one, have attempted to carry out that mission. Most have received that cooperation in the beginning only to have that support erode as more and more decisions, which had to be made for the advancement of the court, alienated enough of the judges that the senators chose to change the chief.

One of the most divisive issues facing the court was the role of the court administrator. Most judges resented this position, because it evolved into a position of great power. In fact, for a while the court administrator was the de facto chief magistrate. The administrator took the position that he controlled the staff and advised them that they were to take orders from him and not from the judges. Efforts by the judges to rein in this authority were met by political resistance and intimidation of the judges who challenged the administrator's role.

Several times, I had been asked to serve as chief. However, having seen the difficulties faced by the previous chiefs, I did not desire to take on the challenge. Eventually, because so many of the judges had common grievances, especially with the escalating power of the court administrator, the majority of the judges convinced me to accept the appointment. I did not seek the position, the other judges convinced the senators to recommend me to the chief justice.

I already knew my term would be limited. No matter how popular a chief was at the beginning of his term, eventually his support would erode. I was, therefore, not surprised when Terry Leverette of Court Administration called and told me he was "going to put a target on my back" by announcing my appointment as chief magistrate.

My first order of business was to eliminate the position of court administrator. With the help of Karen Kanes Floyd, who was now the Chairman of Spartanburg County Council, much was achieved. I cannot take the whole credit, since without Karen's complete support, the finances would not have been available. With her efforts, the council supported long overdue upgrades to our physical facilities. A new wing was remodeled for our civil division, giving much needed space and an additional courtroom. Computers were upgraded and the district judges offices were computerized with high speed internet for the first time.

New judges were added to the jail to help clear the jail by doing more frequent arraignments. The cost savings paid for their positions. Again with Karen's help, we increased the district judges salaries by fifty percent – the highest salary increase before or since. This was done by increasing their hours in their district offices. They were paid by the number of hours worked, so it vastly increased their salaries and, more importantly, provided greater access for the public to judicial services throughout the county.

Spartanburg had never had an associate chief magistrate. I asked the chief justice to appoint Ed Overcash to this position. Ed was invaluable to me. He set up reporting requirements for the judges to insure that cases were being disposed of quickly. With his assistance in assigning judges hours, the competition for extra hours was brought under control. He used his technology skills to establish the first ever website for the court – which continues in use today. Overcash became very active in the South Carolina Summary Court Judges Association, holding several offices including eventually the Presidency of the organization.

Throughout our term, no judge received negative articles in the local press. On the contrary, many positive articles were published in the local papers. More importantly, no judge during this period received any disciplinary action for wrongdoing. While others will have to judge our performance, this last achievement is the one for which I am most proud. We tried to lead by example, and , at least for a while this worked.

Subsequent chief magistrates have attempted to continue to define their role. Fortunately, as new judges came onto the court, they were more accepting of the role of the chief. Perhaps the most valuable example was the darkest days of the court. When the publicity of the abuses committed by Johnny Cash during his term as chief came to light, others were clear that the choice of chief was even more important to avoid such behavior in the future.

With the election of new senators ,who themselves set out to work together to make the court better, with the choice of new judges, and with the efforts of the existing judges to work together for the good of the court, everyone has benefitted with a stronger court. The role of the chief magistrate has been made easier with this common goal accepted by all. This does not mean that the chief is not challenged with the limitations of a lean budget. However, the judges have learned that the old ideas of divide and conquer backfired. By supporting the efforts of the chief, they know now that everyone benefits, including those for whom the court is set up to serve.

CHAPTER ELEVEN

Chapter 11 - Surrender those Civil Rights

Chapter 11   Surrender those Civil Rights

Most people today get their impression of judges from popular television shows. The first such offering was "The People's Court". Judge Wapner, to his credit held to the ethical standards that we as judges must uphold. As a consequence, the show to many was dull and lifeless . Later shows including a very popular female judge became more lively.

Judges on these shows make rude and disparaging remarks to the litigants. People love it and the shows ratings are high. The average person thinks a judge can do or say anything that they want. They are all powerful. It makes good entertainment.

In reality, judges, including magistrates, are under one of the strictest ethical codes of any profession. The Code of Judicial Conduct has only a few "canons". But these declarations are very powerful and they are subject to much discussion and debate at continuing education seminars. Facts are often presented that lead to many different conclusions as to how a judge should act under certain circumstances.

The difficulty with this is that it makes it hard for judges to determine the right course of conduct in some cases. They may obtain advisory opinions from a panel appointed to issue these advisory ethical opinions. But in the end, the judge is on his or her own to make judgments on how to behave. If a complaint is filed, there is a chance that the Judicial Disciplinary counsel might seek sanctions against the judge which could end a career.

Some things are obvious. Insulting remarks about a person's intelligence or weight are clearly prohibited in real life though not on television. Memberships in organizations that discriminate or exclude people due to race is clearly prohibited. Other things are much more fuzzy.

Judges are prohibited from engaging in political activity unless they are campaigning for a judgeship. This means a judge cannot contribute to a political party or individual candidate. Judges may not attend political debates that are open to the public to acquaint themselves with a candidate's position on important issues. Certainly, the judge cannot display political signs in his yard or bumper stickers on his vehicle.

What happens, however, if the judge's wife or son becomes a candidate for political office. Do the same prohibitions apply such that he cannot attend a speaking engagement for his relative? There is some debate on this, but most opinions appear to prohibit the judge from supporting the candidacy in any public way.

A judge cannot write a letter to the editor of a newspaper expressing an opinion on a controversial issue. They cannot write a letter of recommendation for another. Neither can they lend their name to the most noble of fundraising efforts. The list goes on and on to the extent that a judge basically forfeits his or her civil rights upon ascending to the bench.

These prohibitions are hard on a judge but even more so on his family. The wife or kids have trouble understanding why the judge cannot engage in activities other husbands and fathers take for granted. This is understandable and has led at times to regrets for the profession that I chose. But in the end, like the families of soldiers, the people you care about adapt and accept the limitations.

A judge never stops being a judge. Even on vacation or on days off, those that see him would lose confidence in the judge's ability to decide the fate of others if they see him intoxicated or telling offcolor jokes. For this reason, some people who possess the legal knowledge, intelligence, or experience choose not to sacrifice their freedom to become a judge.

CHAPTER TWELVE
Chapter 12 - Community standards

Some of the more common types of cases handled in magistrate court are discussed in another chapter. However, some of the most interesting and controversial areas of law dealt with involved vice offenses. Illegal gambling occurred in areas around the county referred to as "ballticket houses". Balltickets were a type of gambling system in which parties placed bets on the outcome of athletic events. Everyone in law enforcement knew where these ticket houses were, but unless they had gotten an undercover officer or an informant to buy some tickets, they could not search the premises. Each time the sheriff hired new officers, for a time he would use them in an undercover capacity to try and get the evidence needed to search. Therefore, search warrants were sought quite frequently for these places of gambling.

Shortly after I came on the court, the sheriff established his first vice unit. It consisted of two officers and a supervisor. One of the officers chosen was a person who had in his earlier years often frequented places around the county where illegal liquor was sold. These places offered both illegally manufactured liquor known as "moonshine" or lawful liquor sold without being licensed to sell it. Most often these places sold the liquor at times when legal liquor stores were closed.

With the officer's prior experience with these liquor houses, he was successful in making purchases which violated the law.

Additionally, his prior lifetime experiences got him into the ballticket houses, and he made many illegal gambling cases. The officer became so successful at his job that word spread quickly and he began having trouble making buys.

Attention then turned to another area of vice that had attracted public attention. In the early 1970's pornographic movies had begun popping up on outdoor movie screens at formerly popular drive-in theatres. The drive-in theatre had been a very popular family entertainment source during my youth.The entire family could enjoy the latest Disney movie or Elvis Presley movie at one of several such outdoor theatres.

Unfortunately, with the invention of cable television and the vcr, it became cheaper and more convenient for the family to enjoy these movies in their own home. As a result , attendance at drive-ins started diminishing. They began offering "B" movies, horror movies, and other types of genres that attracted young people, and this extended their life for a few more years. However, attendance continued to taper off until they seized on the newly emerging porno movie industry.

The movies "Deep Throat" and "Behind the Green Door" became national sensations in the "love child" era of the late 1960's and early 1970's . Anti pornography laws were passed to prohibit the exhibition of sexually explicit movies that violated " community standards" of decency. The drive-in theaters began to test the waters on these community standards as their audiences swelled to see the new movie fare. Accordingly, one night the vice squad came to see me and said they had gotten complaints on a popular drive-in. They wanted a search warrant to shut the theater down.

In these early days, establishing "probable cause" to search for and seize the movie presented challenges to both law enforcement and the courts. There would be no way that a judge could preview the movie without actually watching it and he could only watch it at the theater. Therefore, with blank search warrant in hand, I got in the back seat of the vice squad's vehicle and we headed for the show. On the way one of the officer's said, "I need to give you a heads up. There is a little dirt road that goes behind a motel beside the drive-in. We will enter there and you might be surprised at what you see." Sure enough, as we came around the back of the motel, lined up on the dirt road were a series of marked police vehicles of various police agencies around the area. As we approached, one by one, they started up and pulled away. Apparently, the interest level was high in what we were about to see.

Upon entering the drive-in, we pulled up to one of the speaker stands and put the speaker in the window to hear. The movie began and, after awhile, it was clear that what had been shown violated local community standards. I had written in the affidavit facts supporting probable cause to search for and seize the film. When I offered the document to the vice officer to sign, he said, "Judge, we have to be sure the movie violates the law. Let's watch a little more!" About an hour later, he signed the warrant and we approached the projection booth.

After the warrant was served, the employee announced over his intercom, "We have been raided. The movie is over." We could hear a parade of cars starting up and leaving as the projectionist rewound the film on a large wooden table and placed it in a large metal carrying case. This continued about every three months for about a year until the theaters stopped showing the adult films and returned to their fare of horror films.

By this time a series of small shops had opened up which were referred to as "peep shows". These shops offered movies on 8 mm film. The customer would deposit a sum of money into the projector and peep into a viewer to watch a few minutes of the film. Most of these films had no sound but they were clearly of a sexual nature. The films were also offered for sale. Therefore, the vice officers began purchasing the movies and bringing them to me to establish probable cause for search warrants.

My wife had no idea the use my 8 mm projector would be put to when I bought it to show movies of our kids. When my wife and children were tucked safely in bed, I would begin the "burden" of viewing the evidence to determine probable cause for a warrant. This continued on for sometime. I later learned that prosecutors had to view some of these movies several times before they were certain they had cases they could win. I learned that after the cases were over the movies often got distributed and were being shown at local parties. One day I was about to preside over a preliminary hearing on a pornography case and was told that another judge who was on vacation had the evidence in the trunk of his car.

Another crime that started causing concern in the community was that of prostitution. This age old profession had been practiced for centuries in quiet seclusion. It had for the most part been ignored since it was not out in the open. However, a series of businesses began opening what were called "massage parlors". While body massage was legal, more intimate sexual contact in exchange for money was the nature of illegal prostitution.

Because these businesses were so visable and because complaints by neighbors and others began increasing, the vice squad set out to investigate these businesses. Most of them offered for sale "sexual toys" and movies. Some even had a peep show room attached. Arrests began to be made for prostitution. I was in the booking room one evening when the police identification officer was asking one of the girls under arrest about her clients. She boldly bragged, "My clients include, doctors, lawyers, and some of the most prominent people in Spartanburg." Unfortunately, the police had not found her client register.

Eventually, both the peep shows and the massage parlors left the area. However, a new chapter began when a local "madam" started opening a series of "escort services". She represented that she simply offered a dating service. A scandal broke when the local paper reported allegations that many police officers were providing "protection" to the madam in exchange for "dates". This protection manifested itself in the form of warnings when raids were about to occur. After this exposure and a few convictions, the madam agreed to cease her escort service business.

When I was in high school in the 1960's illegal drugs were barely known. The most serious offense a student could commit was smoking cigarettes in the restroom. By the time I became a judge in the early 1970's heavy drugs still were not prevalent in our community. The hippie generation and the pop music culture made marijuana and LSD popular on the West Coast and in more metropolitan areas. Of these, only marihuana had crept into our area in the early 70's. Gradually, this changed, until the vice squads expanded and a joint city-county drug task force was formed.

Our activity at night exploded as raids were made or undercover sting operations netted dozens of defendants resulting in the need for hundreds of warrants. Both my secretary and I would frequently spend the entire night preparing warrants, doing arraignments, and executing appearance bonds for the release of those charged. One evening we remained until three o'clock in the morning processing one such raid.

An event that still strikes horror in the heart of my friend Larry Powers, the former director of the Spartanburg Detention Facility, was known as the "July Jam". A promoter decided to hold a hard rock concert at a local drive-in theater that had closed. The event was to be an all day concert on a Saturday in early July. Upon hearing of the event, the sheriff issued a warning in the local paper that his officers would be out in full force and would enforce the laws against public intoxication and other vice activities.

At the time, the jail was a part of the main courthouse. There was an upstairs corridor that led into the courthouse, and below was a breezeway that led to the entrance to the magistrate court. I received a call at about eight o'clock that evening from my chief magistrate. He asked if I could come to the jail and help arraign some people. He described the atmosphere as a "zoo". When I arrived, it was still light outside and as I crossed the breezeway entrance to the jail I saw broken glass from the windows above.

Upon entering the jail, the zoo- like atmosphere was obvious . People were everywhere. All the cells were full. People were in the stairways, in the hallways, and in the outside exercise area which was enclosed with a fifteen foot high chain link fence. Officers were in riot gear and carried nightsticks. Several judges had been called in to help. Food had been exhausted and the jail was down to "kool aid" and peanut butter sandwiches. Prisoners were throwing bodily fluids and the sandwiches at the officers. The chain link fence in the recreation area was being rocked back and forth and the officers expected it to break.

It was a crisis and we set out to solve it. The jail had a booking area that was about twenty by thirty feet long. We had four judges working in the jail, so we lined people up in groups of 10-15 and advised them en masse of their rights. Those that wanted to plead guilty we accepted and sentenced them either to the small amount of money they possessed or gave them "time served". The county administrator had been advised of the problem and he came to help.

He was assigned to reissue the persons their personal effects that had been taken from them. Those people were sent on their way. Those that wanted a trial were sent over to another judge in our office to prepare a bond form for trial.

A local television crew arrived at the fence outside and began interviewing the prisoners. The story aired for days on television and in the local newspaper. Law suits were threatened. Fortunately, things calmed down after a few days. Trials were set for some but were not prosecuted since the officers could not remember who they had arrested and for what charge. Even today, when Larry Powers and I discuss the "old days", a mention of the July Jam causes the blood to drain from his face.

CHAPTER THIRTEEN
Chapter 13 - Types of cases heard

Criminal cases.

Traditionally, magistrates have been the place where "minor " criminal offenses have been heard. Those who are victims and often those who are defendants don't see any case as "minor". When people's lives are affected, the case is major to them. Therefore, "minor" simply means that the penalty after conviction is not that great. No death penalty trials are decided in magistrate court , although I have had many people appear in court who have considered it "life or death".

The traditional maximum penalty upon conviction is thirty days in jail or a fine. The fine has ranged from twenty-five dollars up to the present maximum of five hundred dollars. In recent times, magistrates have been given jurisdiction over offenses that carry a larger than five hundred dollar fine and some that carry a fine and possible jail time. This is a departure from the historical tradition of a fine or imprisonment. Due to an ever expanding caseload in the higher courts, magistrate courts have had to absorb more serious offenses in recent years. All of this skews the traditional concept that magistrates hear "minor " offenses.

Spartanburg and some of the other larger counties have also developed a "transfer court" in recent years. This is a special division of the magistrate court where the circuit solicitor with consent of a criminal defendant will transfer the case to be heard into this special division of magistrate court. Penalties cannot exceed one year imprisonment. This helps remove cases from the circuit court and provides a speedier disposition. Victims receive restitution sooner, so overall it benefits the whole system.

The two most serious offenses heard in magistrate court are driving under the influence and criminal domestic violence. Even though vastly different types of offenses, these have some common consequences. The most serious is the fact that the crime can multiply into second, third, and subsequent offenses. Most offenses in magistrate court don't multiply.

The second common characteristic is that the offenses take a while to be removed from a person's record. Expungement is a process by which criminal convictions are removed from a person's criminal history. Most offenses can be expunged in magistrate court after one year. At one time, criminal domestic violence convictions could not be expunged at all. Today, it can be after several years. Driving under the influence offenses fall off the record after ten years.

Another common characteristic of these two offenses are the collateral consequences of convictions. In the case of driving under the influence, it manifests itself in a special kind of costly insurance that must be carried for three years after conviction. Additionally, a convicted DUI offender must attend a type of counseling class on the dangers of alcohol use, conducted by the local Alcohol and Drug Abuse Commission (ADSAP).

Domestic violence offenders can no longer possess firearms and must attend a special counseling program conducted by organizations approved by the Department of Social Services. Inability to own a firearm, obviously, prevents convicted offenders from engaging in many occupations. Counseling causes conflicts with work schedules and for many people is difficult financially.

The final common characteristic between the offenses is the size of the fines which range anywhere from just under $1000.00 to over $2500.00 defending on a number of factors. Thus, these offenses could in no way be considered "minor".

Historically, magistrate courts have heard crimes that fall into categories. Property crimes and personal injury type crimes along with traffic offenses have been the most common categories of cases heard in these courts. Property crimes involving a limited amount of loss are set to be heard in the magistrate system. The dollar amount has gradually increased over the years. Very recently, the amount was set at two thousand dollars.

Personal injury offenses have most commonly been common law assault or assault and battery. Very recently, many of the crimes created at common law were abolished by legislation in South Carolina. What I have known most of my legal career as common law assault is now " third degree assault".

Traffic offenses are the ones most people are familiar with. Most drivers sometimes in their lives will most likely get a speeding ticket. Other offenses involve minor accidents or licensing issues for the person or their vehicle. Every conviction removes points from their driving license and has the collateral consequence of causing their liability insurance rates to be raised. Since most people need their license to get to work , to school, to soccer practice, or hundreds of other places, these offenses don't seem minor to the accused.

Intoxication from alcohol is the root cause of many people having to appear in magistrate court. An officer could spend his entire shift just transporting publicly intoxicated people to jail. One officer who became the subject of ridicule by his fellow officers would sign onto the radio at the beginning of his shift and make it his goal to call in an arrest of a drunk within five minutes. His fellow officers used to have a betting pool as to the exact minute and second he would make that first call to dispatch.

Most officers knew that they could roust people in what they called the "green leaf hotel", being the woods, bridge underpasses, and other common public areas. However, if the person appeared to be safe, they would leave him alone. Even in those cases where intoxication arrests were made of regular defendants, the officers more often than not would not show up for court. They knew the case would be dismissed, but they felt they had done their job by causing the person to sober up .

Upon conviction, judges most often would sentence the defendant to "time served". This is because they knew these people had no money and the cell space was needed for other prisoners. Additionally, housing an alcoholic person in jail was an expense to the taxpayer that most often than not could not be recouped.

Growing up I enjoyed a popular comedian Red Skelton. He

played a character he called "Freddie the Freeloader", who was an alcoholic. When the weather got bad or when holidays arrived, Freddie would most likely be in jail where he was safe. I recall an episode where Freddie tried and tried to get arrested, but it being Christmas Eve, the officer kept excusing his conduct. Finally, Freddie went to the jail and hit the jailer with his shoe. He got what he wanted.

Similar events occurred in real life. As the weather got colder or when special holiday meals were on tap at the jail, the regulars sometimes had to find a way to "break into jail". Officers, jailers, and magistrates tried to accommodate these folks, realizing the consequences otherwise. We often worried when some of our regulars did not show up for awhile. I remember asking, "Where is Whoopie?" after not seeing one of our weekend regulars for several weeks.

It is not common for judges to receive praise. On the contrary, many people like to criticize judges and their decisions. On a few rare occasions, I would run into someone who would say, "I know you don't remember me, but you changed my life. You put me in jail for a week and told me to reflect on my life. After hitting bottom, I did just that. I sobered up, went back to school, and now I have a good job and family. I owe much of this to you!" Unfortunately, these events have been far too infrequent.

When I began people were put in jail and unless they paid out or someone came to check on them they stayed there for days, weeks, or even months before trial or release on bail. After the Judicial Reform Amendment the new Court Administration under orders from the chief justice established a requirement for arraignment of arrested persons. This was required to be done at least every twelve hours.

So in Spartanburg we began doing this at least once on every shift. Since the jail was next door to the magistrate office this was not difficult. I did this early in my shift and again about halfway through the night. This helped relieve the jail from keeping people too long.

The arraignment was a process by which the judge advised the defendants of the charges against them and the possible penalties if convicted. Then the judge determined if the person could be released on his own recognizance meaning signing a bond to guarantee their appearance in court. If they did not qualify, then a security bond amount was set that had to be signed by a property owner to guarantee appearance by the defendant.

Additionally, the defendant was to be advised of his right to an attorney, the right to a trial by jury and how to request it, and the right to a preliminary hearing if the case would be tried in the higher court. The judge had to fill out a checklist in writing that all of this was done.

As long as the jail was next door this was fine. However, a few years after I began a new jail was built several miles from the courthouse. This presented a problem since judges would have to leave the courthouse and go to the jail for arraignment which at night disrupted the availability for a judge at the courthouse.

Accordingly, with the help of county council and the leadership of Judge Overcash Spartanburg was the first in the upstate to set up video arraignments. Equipment was installed at the jail and the courthouse so the judge could talk to the prisoners from the courthouse and do the arraignment.

Before this could be done the chief justice had to give approval. Therefore, former Chief Justice Bruce Littlejohn of Spartanburg came by and asked me if he could sit in on my evening arraignments. He did this and I showed him how well this worked so he recommended this to the current chief justice and we began the process.

A few years later the equipment went bad and the cost of replacement was high. By that time as chief magistrate I had gotten approval for judges around the clock at the jail. Accordingly, the video process was no longer needed.

About ten years later the Greenville magistrate court claimed to be the first in the upstate to do video arraignments and had the press promote this falsehood. Spartanburg had done this ten years before.

Civil Cases.

The civil caseload in magistrate court has traditionally consisted of two main types of cases. These are landlord-tenant cases and cases in claim and delivery. Most everyone knows what landlord-tenant cases are since most of us have rented a place to live at some time in our lives. Claim and delivery is a procedure where the owner of personal property is attempting to retrieve that property from another person who refuses to give it up. The property has to have been lawfully placed in the hands of the person in possession such as a neighbor loaning his lawnmower to another neighbor. Upon demand, the neighbor in possession refuses to give it back to the owner, so the owner comes to magistrate court to get an order of repossession.

Another common occurrence would be when an item was sold by a store and the purchaser stopped paying for the item. In such instance, the seller would want to get the merchandise back. Additionally, it was common for people to approach small loan companies for money and pledge personal property as collateral. Upon the failure of the debtor to repay the loan, the lender would seek claim and deliver to get the collateral.

If the person seeking repossession won the case they would be awarded an order to seize the property or , in the alternative, a judgment for the value of the property. A court constable would be sent to assist the owner in recovering the property in question. Until recent years, the central magistrate court handled many of these cases and set aside a regular day and time each week to handle hundreds of such cases. Today, most of the businesses realize that getting back the collateral in most cases is not worth the effort. Therefore, the caseload has diminished significantly.

In the landlord-tenant matters, there has been no similar decrease in caseload. Each week on the same day and time, the courtroom is overflowing with landlords and tenants. Most often the reason for eviction is non payment of rent. Other reasons are sometimes pled and the issues are heard. In the event an eviction is ordered the constable must serve notice on the tenant that it will be carried out within twenty-four hours of service of the notice. If the tenant does not vacate, the constable supervises as the landlord sets the tenant's property on the roadside.

The magistrate court also has handled and does handle a wide variety of other civil disputes such as minor automobile accidents, breaches of contract, non payment of wages, and many other disputes within the dollar jurisdiction of the court. This has increased steadily over the years from just a few dollars to a maximum of $7500.00 today. One major exception to this limit is that magistrates are granted unlimited dollar jurisdiction in landlord-tenant matters. This really only comes into play in actions to collect unpaid rent . This process allows the magistrate to determine the unpaid amount of rent and authorize his constable to inventory and sell at public auction personal property found on the rented premises. Several times, we have collected rent in excess of one hundred thousand dollars through this process.

CHAPTER FOURTEEN
Chapter 14 - How magistrates are paid

As judges of the Civil and Criminal Court our salary was set at a percentage of a circuit judge's salary. This was an easy method to calculate. As mentioned earlier, I often worked many more hours than I was paid for, but I knew that when I took the job. It was really not hard to do, since I loved the job after serving for a very short time. Accordingly, I never complained about my pay.

It was not so simple for the part-time magistrates in the districts around the county. Each one was assigned to a territorial area and the caseload reflected the area the judge was serving. An area like Inman being more populated and having a larger town inside the magistrate's district would have a heavier caseload than a more rural district.

These part-time magistrates were paid by the caseload. Accordingly, the more cases handled the larger the salary. The potential for abuse in such a system is obvious. At the time I began as a judge, there was a particular magistrate that would always write a "breach of peace" warrant no matter what other warrant he issued. He effectively doubled his caseload and consequentially his salary. This continued for quite some time until he issued a murder warrant and the breach of peace warrant. The defendant's attorney said to the judge, "I will plead my client guilty to the breach of peace if you dismiss the murder warrant." The duplicate warrant issuance ended shortly thereafter.

More troubling was the common practice of highway patrol officers to "judge shop". This is the practice of finding a court where they would get the most favorable results. If a magistrate ruled against him in a case, the trooper would threaten to take his cases elsewhere. This would be devastating to the judge's salary. Accordingly, this process had a chilling effect on justice.

Eventually, the Supreme Court struck down the practice of paying by caseload and ordered that a system be devised to set a fair salary structure for part-time magistrates. As chief magistrate, Judge Edward Overcash set forth to devise a means of doing this. He took a percentage of a full time judge's salary and worked out a formula for an hourly wage. By consultation with county council the number of hours a magistrate would work in their offices each week was determined. Multiplying this by the hourly wage produced the salary.

Unfortunately, this did not settle the issue. Some judges believed that they should get more hours in their offices. They would cite increasing numbers of cases coming into their courts and put constant pressure on the chief magistrate to increase their hours. Some areas entered agreements with towns to provide a magistrate for several hours a week to handle their cases. These were districts in which a larger town existed. Agreements were entered between county council and the towns to do this and so these judges got a few more hours each week. Some of those that did not have these towns still pressed the chief magistrate to increase their hours.

Even more difficult was the assigning of judges to the "jail referral" duty. This set off a battle between some of the judges to get these hours and the hourly pay for these duties. Working an eight hour shift paid as much as a whole week in one's office. There developed two groups – those that wanted to work and those that did not. Those that wanted to work often reached an agreement with those that did not that when the judge's name showed on the schedule that did not want to work a particular judge automatically worked that schedule.

This led to jealousies and infighting. Some judges tried to intimidate newer judges who came onto the court into giving up their hours. Other methods of persuasion were tried and it became a very ugly process. It was not behavior that a judge should be involved in.

When I became chief magistrate, one of my first goals was to end this unseemly practice. Fortunately, the year 2000 census helped solve the problem. Spartanburg would get two new fulltime magistrate positions. By law these positions had to be filled. However, the fulltime positions could be divided into four part-time positions.

We utilized one of the fulltime positions to create four judges at the jail. We had a second and third shift fulltime judge already assigned through the week. By adding a part-time judge on first shift, it freed the judges at the courthouse from having to do arraignments so they could devote more time to trials. Arraignments could be done more frequently, and by getting people with minor offenses out of the jail sooner, the cost savings paid for the new judge.

More importantly, we were able to have judges covering the jail on weekends and holidays on each shift. There would be no more fighting over hours with the requisite hard feelings. The staff at the jail would work with the same judge all the time, so they did not have to learn the habits of several different judges. The county was going to have to pay for the new judges anyway, but by utilizing them in this manner, no new offices had to be rented, no additional utility bills were generated, and the judges did not need additional secretaries or constables. The overall savings to the county were good.

However, I recognized that those judges who had come to rely on the extra income by working at the jail would be upset. Therefore, I convinced county council to increase the magistrates' hours in their offices by six hours each week. This benefitted the communities by having judges available more frequently. It increased the part-time judges salaries by fifty percent (the largest salary increase before or since) and it was paid for by the savings of the jail operation. This resulted in a more professional court and more efficiency in cost.

In the year 2000, the magistrate reform bill was passed. One of the issues addressed was the pay for judges across the state. A plan was devised to pay them a percentage of a circuit judge's salary. The percentage was greater in larger populated counties. The law provided that a judge's pay could not be reduced during his term in office. However, the bill provided that a county could pay a higher salary and benefits to a magistrate than provided by the bill.

Across the state, this bill raised many magistrate's salaries substantially. In Spartanburg, it had little effect. Most of Spartanburg's magistrates salaries exceeded the formula. This was because when the judges of the Civil and Criminal Court became the courthouse magistrates again, they kept the salaries that they had. Over the years with annual cost-of-living increases and merit raises (a thing of the past now), Spartanburg's fulltime magistrates salaries were the largest in the state. When Judge Overcash devised his pay plan for part-time magistrates, it was based on the salary of fulltime magistrates, thus making the part-time magistrates benefit.

Since Spartanburg's magistrates have been men and women of great character, dedication, and legal skills, they have developed a very positive reputation throughout the state. To get and keep professional people, the salary structure must reflect this. In our county it does.

CHAPTER FIFTEEN

Chapter 15 - The People

Since the magistrate court is often referred to as the "people's court", a few examples of the people that have appeared in court will help illustrate this designation. The reason the court is referred to in this manner is that, most often, people represent themselves in magistrate court. In modern time more and more lawyers have started practicing in these courts. But in the early days it was rare to have a lawyer show up on a case.

Many of you may remember a popular television program called "Night Court". Judge Harry Anderson presided over a comic array of cases in his evening court. For over eighteen years, I was Harry Anderson, presiding over Spartanburg's version of "night court" with the exception there was no Markie Post. There was no prosecutor, public defender or bailiff in the vast majority of cases.

Judge Ellen Smith told me on my first day that people "crawled out from under rocks at night". There certainly were "different" people who appeared in my court than appeared during the day. Since most magistrates held their court at night, they experienced similar results.

Since the magistrate's job traditionally had been to help people with their problems no matter what the problem the local police would advise "go see the magistrate". I actually had people come in to report UFO sightings. Most men worked during the day and when they got home domestic disputes began to occur. An elderly gentlemen came in one night and wanted papers to reclaim his false teeth from his wife who had gotten mad at him and hidden them.

Although not an official part of a magistrate's job, more and more people showed up wanting to get married. Either the probate court which normally performed this service was closed or a minister would not marry them because one of them had been divorced. Whatever the reason, over my career I have probably married more than five hundred couples. I developed a non religious ceremony and it seemed to satisfy the parties.

Police officers often asked for my help. I actually married one ranking officer to the same woman three different times. Another got this service four times but with different women. Once I married a couple, was later asked to represent them in a mutually agreeable divorce, and two years later remarried them.

The most unique event was a couple who came in one night and asked to be married. She was in full wedding gown. The groom was in a tuxedo as were his and her fathers. I married them and then took then over to the jail for a series of comic photos. One of these had him in the holding cell at the jail with the wife trying to open the door.

A week later the new groom came in one night in a panic. He said his new wife had tried to kill him with a knife. I thought he was not being truthful until he brought her father in to confirm the truth of his claim. I learned that they had gotten an annulment shortly thereafter. However, most of the marriages seemed to have a better outcome.

Real life characters were oftentimes more interesting than the comics who appeared on television shows like "Night Court" and the popular "Andy Griffith Show". We had our "Otis Campbells" or town drunks. One such was a pair of twins who were hardworking housepainters through the week but ended up in jail each weekend. Another was a fellow who when drunk would shout out loudly "Whoopee!". A weekend regular guest was a fellow who had lost both his legs and arms when a train ran over him. He certainly had a reason to become intoxicated which he regularly did. Though really sad, it was hard to hold back a laugh when he would enter the jail and have his wheel chair taken away. He would run round and round on the stumps of his arms and legs challenging the officers to a fight.

One of the most interesting characters was a lady we will call Precious. I was told the story by my father when I was sent to defend her neighbor who we will call Mr. Brown while I was still practicing law. Twenty five years earlier my grandfather had represented Precious's husband in a divorce. Apparently, she had irritated him for so long that he had loaded his shotgun with bird shot and blown her off the toilet. Even though her physical injuries were not that severe, she certainly suffered a shock to her pride, and she got the divorce she was entitled to.

There were no children of the marriage and the only property was the house and lot they lived in and an adjacent undeveloped lot. Precious got the house and her husband got the undeveloped lot. He promptly deeded this to my grandfather as his fee. Shortly thereafter, my grandfather sold the lot to Mr. Brown, and , to his eternal regret, Mr. Brown built a house and began living next to Precious.

The police were called hundreds of times over the following years by Precious complaining about Mr. Brown. Precious had the phone company put a twenty foot cord on her phone so she could go out on her porch and ask the police to listen to the noises being generated by her neighbor. The police and older members of the Spartanburg Bar who knew the story would stir her up just to see her reaction. She was a legend around the courthouse.

So my father sent me to defend Mr. Brown in a jury trial in the Civil and Criminal Court where Brown was charged with "breach of peace". Precious initially was represented by over five of Spartanburg's most prominent lawyers. Someone actually tried to get The Charlotte Observer newspaper to cover the story. One by one the lawyers withdrew from the case until Precious was left to her own devices. Even so, the courtroom was overflowing with spectators on the date of the trial.

Precious presented the officer who responded to her complaint who testified he did not see or hear anything. He acknowledged on my cross examination that he was routinely called by Precious and never found any evidence of a crime. Then Precious took the stand. She testified to the long history of problems with Mr. Brown. She presented her medal for twenty-five years of attendance at her local church. She also offered a copy of a petition she said Mr. Brown had presented to her neighbors resulting in her being "excommunicated" from her church.

My job was relatively easy since the jury could easily see the complaint for what it was. After five minutes of deliberation, Mr. Brown was found "not guilty". Unfortunately, Precious did not go away easily. After becoming a judge, every Sunday morning I would get a call from her complaining about noise from a junkyard just down the street. I envisioned her with the twenty- foot phone cord stretched to the limit as she implored in that high pitched voice "Do you hear that?". Then she would begin a twenty minute tirade about how no one would help her. I would place the phone on "hold" and return ever so often as she was still rattling away like a machine gun. Eventually, she would give up and free my line.

A young man who we will call Hippie Smith was the son of a prominent Spartanburg citizen. Hippie experimented with a number of the popular street drugs of the time to such an extent that his mind had become affected. At times he was very lucid and at other times he was barely understandable. When his father died, his mother became his guardian. He would walk the streets and stay out all night often. Frequently, he would be arrested for various minor offenses.

One evening around eleven o'clock, Hippie's mother came in to see if he was in jail. I called and asked to have him brought to our office. She paid his bond and he came in and told her that there was a friend in jail he wanted to help get released. When she refused to pay him out, he asked if he could use our phone to call his friend's "old lady". I asked "What is your friend's name?" He replied, "I only know him as "Laid Back". I handed him the phone and he dialed the number. When someone answered, he said, " Hello, Mrs. Laid Back!". It was all I could do to keep from rolling on the floor, when he looked at me with a puzzled expression "She hung up on me!" he said.

People's behavior was often predictable. Property crimes increased, for example, during certain times of the year. As Christmas approached there would be an increase in shoplifting and two weeks after Christmas, the fraudulent checks poured in. In the era up to the turn of the twenty- first century, one annual event influenced the increase in property crimes. Each October, the Piedmont Interstate Fair became the place to go. Numerous games of chance dominated the fairgrounds and it seemed like every young man wanted to win his girl a giant teddy bear. Although no studies were ever done on the relationship of this event to the concurrent increase in property crimes to most the coincidence seemed predictable.

It has often been said that holidays cause many to become depressed. As a result, having worked every Christmas for several years, I had to issue a murder warrant every time. Additionally, I am one who believes in the influence of the full moon on human behavior. Police officers would often comment "Their will be a shooting tonight.", as the moon shown full in the sky. The word "lunatic" is a derivative from the word "lunar" meaning "moon". After many years on the job, I may not believe in werewolves, but I do believe in the effect of the full moon on human behavior.

One interesting consequence of being a judge and having so many people appear before you, is that you are constantly recognized. Sometimes, people think they should know you but do not remember how they know you. More than once, I have had people in public announce. "I know you. Where do I know you from?". When I respond "You don't want to know." it sometimes does not pursuade them to desist. " Come on, tell me where I know you from?" they insist. Finally, after they have attracted a lot of attention, I have to reply " I put you in jail last year.".

My wife is surprised when we are walking on a public street and a guy driving a vehicle that looks like a "hippie van" from the 1960's yells out loudly "Hey judge!". However, these are my people. If you work in the magistrate court, you must be a "people person". You must love people and understand what motivates them. I have always been conscious of the fact that but for the grace of God and a lot of luck, I could be the guy on the other side of the bench.

CHAPTER SIXTEEN

Chapter 16 - Spartanburg's Most Influential Magistrates in Modern Times

Part A

In other parts of this book magistrates in the early part of Spartanburg County history have been discussed. However, most of the changes and improvements in the magistrate court system began in the mid twentieth century around the 1950s. Some of the judges that helped develop this must be properly recognized. We begin with the person who opened the door for women to serve in these positions.

Ellen Hines Smith

In the early 1970's, females did not yet play a major role in the legal community. This had been and still was a male dominated profession. Although one other female had been the first to serve as a magistrate in Spartanburg County , she did not serve long enough to impact the profession. Ellen Hines Smith did.

Judge Smith was a brilliant woman with high moral and ethical standards. She spent her life working to help those who were less able to help themselves. When I joined the Civil and Criminal Court in 1973, she had been on the court for a couple of years. She had risen to the position of chief judge of the court and served with Wallace Dickerson on the first shift. I joined the court as the night, weekend and holiday judge. Ellen Smith welcomed me and became a mentor and friend. She understood the attitudes of those who thought women should stay at home and raise children. There were many of those both in the public and in the legal profession.

Daily I admired the calm and professional manner in which she deflected the bias directed at her. Sometimes it was even overt. We developed a bond because I received some of the same type of bias due to my age. The prejudice even extended to members of the staff who were not used to having a female boss. It is hard to overstate how radical it was to have a female serving in such a prominent position as a judge.

Because of the environment in which she worked Judge Smith had to and did develop a very thick skin. She was such a warm person that when she was certain she was right against the majority she sometimes seemed unduly stubborn. However, I admired the skill with which she navigated the shark filled waters around her. Her legal skills and instincts were outstanding.

Ellen came from good legal stock. Her father Joseph Hines had been a tough and aggressive federal prosecutor. Her brother Joe was a partner in the prominent law firm of Carlisle Bean and Hines. She had obviously grown up as I in a legal family that instilled a love for the law in her.

At the time a person accused of a crime that went to the higher court known as the Court of General Sessions by statute had a right to a preliminary hearing in the magistrate court. This hearing was to determine if there was probable cause for the case to proceed to trial in the higher court. The law allowed hearsay testimony to be introduced in this hearing. In most courts only hearsay was used. Judge Smith, however, believed that live witnesses must be presented and thus, preliminary hearings became mini trials in the Civil and Criminal Court.

This procedure went on for several years after Judge Smith left the court. It was well liked by the defense bar but prosecutors did not especially like the idea. However, I was involved with two very important cases that were resolved successfully because of this procedure.

The first case was a charge against a person in a series of rape cases involving a person known as the "duck pond rapist". It was common for lovers to stop at a popular site along a major highway adjacent to the Milliken Research Plant which had a duck pond. Suddenly, young women started to be raped at gunpoint by a male who failed to cover his face. Accordingly, a composite drawing was done by one of the victims.

The police staked out the area and caught a person one evening on Milliken property in the vicinity of the duck pond. He looked very much like the composite drawing. He was arrested and charged with the multiple rapes. The case was set for preliminary hearing and I was called in to hear the case since one of the judges was on vacation.

At the preliminary hearing the defendant had been released on bond and sat next to his attorney at counsel table. The young prosecutor sat with the victim of one of the cases at the prosecution table. To better understand this at the time the judge's bench consisted of an old World War II era metal desk on a platform elevated about twelve inches off the floor. Counsel tables were only a couple a feet from the judge's "bench" and separated from one another by only a couple of feet. The courtroom was not much bigger than a good sized bedroom and probably could seat only about thirty people.

A witness chair was set on the raised platform adjacent to the judge. The witness then was only arm's length from the counsel tables. Microphones were not needed because in the small environment there was no problem hearing everything that occurred anywhere in the room.

At the hearing, the prosecutor called the victim as a witness and she testified in detail to the events of the evening in question. She was shown the composite drawing and she stated that fairly represented the perpetraitor . After she finished answering the prosecutor's questions the defense attorney asked her a few more questions about it being dark and how could she be sure of her identification. She was adamant that she got a good look at the person who attacked her and that he held a gun on her and her male companion.

When the defense attorney finished, the young prosecutor indicated he had one more question. "Do you see the person in this courtroom who attacked you?" he asked. She surveyed the room and stared at the defendant sitting only three to four feet from her and replied " No sir." I had no choice but to grant the defense motion to find no probable cause to bind that defendant over for trial.

Two months later, the police caught the real criminal. He confessed to the crimes. As it turned out he was a cousin of the originally charged person and bore a striking resemblance to him. I often wondered had we not had live witnesses at the preliminary hearing would the police have continued to investigate and look for the person who committed these terrible crimes. It clearly seemed that Judge Smith's procedure was correct.

The second case involved a prominent member of the state

House of Representatives. I was called one afternoon by my chief magistrate and asked to come in to consider an application for a warrant. The State Law Enforcement Division had been called in when a man had advised them that a local legislator had been approached to help his son with a parole hearing. The legislator allegedly told the person to bring him some guns and money and his son would get out on parole.

A meeting was arranged and SLED photographed the exchange of guns and money with the lawmaker. SLED was applying for a warrant for bribery. Having reviewed all the evidence I issued the warrant. Immediately, reporters at the local newspaper started a betting pool that I would not send the case forward for trial. I suppose the belief was that political pressure would be brought to bear.

At the preliminary hearing live witnesses laid out the scenario in detail. At the conclusion of the evidence I found probable cause and sent the case forward for trial. The defendant pled to a slightly less serious charge in the higher court. Again, however, without the full live witness procedure I am not sure what would have happened in that case. Judge Smith's judgment was clearly vindicated.

Judge Smith made one critical error that cost her job. Whether she was right or wrong is unclear since I do not know all the facts as she did. She discharged a court constable because he was involved in purchasing some gambling devices known as "ball tickets". He was never charged or convicted of any crime but Judge Smith apparently believed that this brought disfavor on the court.

The constable happened to be a relative of one of Spartanburg County's most powerful senators. He came and requested that Judge Smith reinstate the constable. Several people close to Judge Smith encouraged her to rehire the person but she remained steadfast. At the next appointment cycle she was replaced.

While this was not a blemish on Judge Smith's career she was well within her legal rights to hire and fire any employee at will I am certain she probably second guessed herself many times. Fortunately many people rallied around her and she founded a home for wayward girls known as the Ellen Hines Smith Girls Home. Ellen Smith became the director of Piedmont Legal Services which provided legal services to those who could not afford them.

Perhaps Ellen's most significant contribution was her many

years of service on Spartanburg City Council where she rose to the office of Vice Mayor. Her tireless efforts ensured that all citizens had an ear when it came to issues before the council. She had pioneered the legal profession for young women to come and there have since been many fine women who have patterned themselves after this excellent role model.

The South Carolina Bar Foundation established The Ellen Hines Smith Legal Services Lawyer of the Year Award. This award has been given annually to a member of the bar that has shown exceptional skills and compassion in representing the poor of society.

Mauldin Pearson

Maulden Pearson

As mentioned earlier Spartanburg had two types of magistrates – the City of Spartanburg or courthouse judges and the district judges. Even though the City of Spartanburg was a district it was different in many ways from the other districts. Virtually all the judges in the city district were lawyers. They handled far more cases than the other districts and as a result had secretaries to help while virtually none of the other districts had this help. Virtually no communications were had between the district judges and the City magistrates.

When I was appointed to the city court in 1973 I was the first judge at the city to work nights, weekends and holidays. Most of the district judges worked nights and were on call at times when they were not in their offices.

Before my appointment they had no one to call for help at night or weekends. Afterword they did and one of the first district judges to call for my help was Judge Maulden Pearson from Pacolet district. He and I became good friends and as a result the other district judges began calling for help on legal issues.

Judge Pearson was a truly caring person who wanted to make the right decisions in his cases. He was extremely popular in his community so much so that he served thirty two years as a magistrate. He became like a second father to me and I valued his advice as much as he valued mine.

With his leadership magistrate courts became a more closely tied court system. For the eighteen years that I served as night, weekend and holiday judge the district judges and I worked together as never before had been done. Even after the chief magistrate position was created they continued to communicate with me regularly and I passed issues along to my fellow city judges.

Accordingly, Judge Pearson was a leader in creating a better court system for Spartanburg County and deserves proper recognition for him.

Edward Overcash

Edward H. Overcash, Jr.

Edward Overcash became one of the earliest of chief magistrates in the mid 1980's. I had met him only once prior to his joining the court. He had appeared in my court one night on a minor matter. Upon being appointed chief magistrate, Judge Overcash and I had very little interaction. Occasionally we might meet at shift change and I would be updated on some matters. However, we did not routinely meet. Judge Overcash ran his shift and I ran mine. By then we had a third shift judge in the person of Andrew Hughes. Judge Hughes was a welcome addition to the court, since I did not have to cover that third shift again.

Ed Overcash did not come from a legal background. His father was a Presbyterian minister. I never discussed with Ed why he got interested in law. His background in college was in accounting and statistics. For that reason, he paid close attention to the details of court proceedings. He spent many hours insuring that the records of the court were accurate and he got interested in automating the recordkeeping. As a result, Judge Overcash was able to introduce to the court the use of personal computers.

Overcash became the longest continually serving chief

magistrate on the court. He served for almost eleven years. The last half of his tenure was frought with challenges and growing pains. He was attempting to define this new position of chief magistrate and he met a lot of opposition from the regional magistrates serving outside the courthouse. This was a new concept. Until 1979 and the creation of this position there was very little interaction among the courthouse magistrates and the territorial magistrates. The new system required the chief magistrate to supervise the operation of all the courts. This required an inordinate amount of attention to the personal relations with the other judges. Overcash was focused more on the technical aspects of the court.

To his credit Judge Overcash learned from his mistakes. After he was moved onto the second shift, he had a chance to realize the challenges the other judges faced. Sometimes, there was no clerk on second shift. Most of the regional magistrates worked without clerks. Additionally, even when a clerk was working, the judge had to sometimes answer the phone, fill out bonds, receipt money , and type warrants. He began to see the challenges the other judges faced daily. He repaired the relations with his harshest critic and they became the best of friends.

Edward Overcash's impact on the court was extremely positive. He introduced personal computers into the court for communications, record keeping, and warrant preparation. He began to explore the use of a computer database to store , search , and print records of cases heard. This eventually led to a much more efficient operation. Additionally, he pioneered the use of videoconferencing to do arraignments. Much of this introduction of technology was new to this level of the court system.

After Overcash moved onto the second shift and I moved to the first shift, we both had to adapt to new lifestyles. Ed did an outstanding job covering the second shift and adapting to the new challenges. After a couple of years, one of the daytime judges moved onto another position. This left an opening on first shift. Having repaired his relations with the other judges, he was recommended for the transfer to the first shift position by his former detractors. Ed and I became friends as he and I shared many similar challenges. We both had a love for the law and a desire to see justice done and we shared a common interest in improving technology in the court.

After Overcash, the average time a chief magistrate served was about three years. The demands of the job, changes in the persons serving as senators, and the ever eroding support of fellow judges helped contribute to a rotation of this position. With Ed Overcash's support along with that of the district judges, I accepted the position of chief magistrate in the year 2000. Although I had been approached on prior occasions about taking this job, I had always discouraged those who supported this. Of all the people who had been judges since the creation of this position, I felt I had a better perspective. I knew the toll it took and I was not ready to undergo that challenge.

However, with new challenges facing the court I agreed to accept the appointment. Since I respected Overcash's counsel so much ,I requested that the chief justice appoint him as the first ever Associate Chief Magistrate for Spartanburg County. He was an excellent partner, a wise advisor and a tireless innovator during our term.

With the help of Ed Overcash, and the assistance of Karen Floyd, who was then the chairman of county council, we achieved many improvements to the system. Ed's early pioneering in database recordkeeping led us to acquire a system that served us well for many years to come. Thanks to help from Karen and the council, we expanded the database bringing all the district magistrates into the new technology. As mentioned in another chapter, we upgraded the salaries of the part-time judges and added permanent judges to our satellite office at the jail. We got a brand new wing to house our civil division and the much needed extra courtroom. This was the first major expansion in over ten years.

Overcash had taught himself a computer language that served him well as he created our court website, being one of the first in the state. During this time he also held several offices in the South Carolina Summary Court Judges Association. He and I, along with another judge, attended their annual convention each year, and we expanded our educational budget to get many of our judges to attend this annual event.

He decided to run for the office of president of the association and I was proud to help him be elected as the first judge from Spartanburg to hold that office. Ed upgraded the educational training classes taught at the association sponsored seminars. He also oversaw a rewriting of the bylaws and constitution of the organization. His organizational skills helped improve the organization and he established the first website for the group.

After twenty-five years serving on the court Ed returned to a successful private practice of law. His influence on the court was enduring and the pioneering of technology made Spartanburg always on the cutting edge of the future. The court has forever been improved by his faithful and longtime involvement.

Karen Kanes Floyd

Karen Kanes Floyd

Judge Karen Kanes came onto the court and her impact was immediate. It was impossible to be around her and feel bad. Her energy level was through the roof and her smile and gentle voice were hypnotic. It was obvious that Karen wanted to improve the court or any organization for which she was a part.

After about a year rumors began that she would be appointed as chief magistrate. Karen always held a party when a big announcement was to be made. She had remodeled an old historic farmhouse in the Reidville community. When we received an invitation to a "hoedown" my wife and I arrived dressed as farmers – me in my overalls and straw hat and Fran in her denim dress and pigtails.

The party was wonderful with good food and music. The house was beautiful and very interesting. However, we learned that the rumors were true – she was to be the chief magistrate. She later told me that the chief justice who she met in person was someone reluctant to appoint someone of her youth to the position. If you know Karen you know that even the chief justice was not immune to the charm that emanated from within her.

One of Karen's first orders was to move me off the second shift that I had managed for eighteen and one-half years. She told me that everyone she talked to recommended that she take advantage of my experience and legal skills. While I agreed (that charm was amazing), I knew the biggest problem was that she was going to move Judge Overcash to second shift. He did not want to do that and I felt guilty taking his daytime slot. I was perfectly happy working the second shift. I was a night person. It was very difficult for me to get up early in the morning. So this meant a complete lifestyle change for me as well as him.

Karen was a great organizer. She knew that the wisest leaders never had all the answers. The most successful surrounded themselves with people that did. That was her management style and it was extremely successful. For my part, I was happy to share knowledge and advice when asked. I became a close advisor to Karen and we have remained friends ever since. She has described me as her big brother. I am flattered that she felt that way.

Even in the early 1990's women were still at a disadvantage in the legal community. Ellen Hines Smith had paved the way but there were hurdles still to be overcome. Ellen Smith persuaded people with her intellect and firmness. Karen melted people like butter in her hand. She inspired those around her with her work ethic and set almost impossible goals – most of which were accomplished.

It saddened most of the judges when Karen left the court. She had become friends with most everyone and they all thought of her as a member of the family. Karen herself often said that she could not stay anywhere too long. It was clear that she had higher ambitions. She was elected by the General Assembly as an Administrative Law Judge but never served. I never saw Karen as a person who would like ruling on applications for liquor licenses.

She married a popular owner of a one hundred-year-old funeral home – Gordon Floyd.

Karen ran for and won the position of Chairman of Spartanburg County Council. She was the first ever female chairman and to the date of this publication is the only female to hold this position in Spartanburg County. In that position she was extremely helpful to the court. She recognized the need for new courtrooms for the magistrate court and had that approved. She chaired the Law Enforcement Committee which brought together the sheriff, the solicitor, the public defender, the director of the jail, the chief magistrate and anyone else who could help improve relations between these departments. Ideas for improving data collection and sharing were explored and cooperation was begun with the chief justice which led to participating in the chief justice's early efforts to track cases throughout the state. Her leadership, skill and knowledge helped promote the Spartanburg Magistrate Court as one of the best in the state. Karen was so persuasive that she got me along with almost all other department heads to dress up like female cheerleaders to entertain the county employees at a picnic. After leaving this position she formed her own advertising agency called the Palladian Group which was very successful and she later became the state chairman of the Republican Party. Like Ellen Hines Smith, Karen Kanes Floyd has left an indelible impression on Spartanburg County and its court system. The story of the magistrate court would not be complete without chronicling her influence.

Karry Guillory

Karry Guillory

A young man grew up in a rural area of Louisiana. He swung on the swings over creeks and played with other friends as all young people do. But he was destined for a more challenging future after playing college basketball and graduating from college. He was extremely smart and wanted to learn and work on a challenging future.

Karry ended up serving as both Associate Chancellor and Vice Chancellor at the University of South Carolina Spartanburg. He later became the assistant director of the Department of Juvenile Justice in South Carolina. After a few years he developed a life threatening cancer which forced him to leave his position at Juvenile Justice. Fortunately, he was treated and recovered completely, proving again he had much to do in the future.

In 2011 Guillory became Judge Guillory after a part-time appointment to the City Magistrate Court at the courthouse. From early on he wanted to learn everything he could about the job. He volunteered to do jobs other judges did not want to do. Since his office was next to mine we talked a lot and he asked me to teach him as much as possible. I was happy to do so and we worked together well as he learned a lot about civil law, evictions and criminal law. He particularly learned the complex case laws dealing with driving under the influence. He volunteered to work at the jail when needed so as to learn bond arraignment procedures.

Judge Guillory became close to the district judges and used his vast skills in management to help them perform better. He also became very close to the staff and was very quickly well liked by the staff. He also developed good relations with law enforcement so that they often sought him out on complicated cases. He also became well respected by lawyers who saw how well he performed in the courtroom.

With Guillory's educational background, he began inviting classes of students in public school and colleges to come and see court in session. Mock trials were developed with other judges with his lead to instill an interest in students in the law. Additionally, he worked on developing training classes for his fellow judges. He convinced speakers to come to Spartanburg to teach classes on gun laws that had previously only been taught in other parts of the state.

Just after my retirement Judge Guillory was appointed as the first fulltime black magistrate to serve in the City Magistrate Court at the courthouse. He fully earned the position and has performed admirably. Recently he was awarded the second highest civilian award given in this state – The Order of the Silver Crescent. Although this book ends at the time of my retirement since not much has changed in the court since then, one exception has occurred. Just before publication of this book Judge Guillory was appointed by the Chief Justice of the South Carolina Supreme Court as the Associate Chief Magistrate in Spartanburg County. This is a truly memorable event since no previous black magistrate has ever held this position.

Spartanburg has for a long time been considered one of the best magistrate courts in the state. It is on a path to continue that tradition with judges like Karry Guillory.

Part B

Three judges as the "Firsts"

These judges were interviewed by Robert B. "Bob" Paslay a longtime newspaper writer and editor of newspapers in Spartanburg, Greenville, Anderson and several across the eastern coast. Bob wrote the following articles about the first black magistrate judge in

Spartanburg since Reconstruction, the first ever black female magistrate, and the first and only Hispanic American judge.

Warren Sullivan, Jr.

A moment of history occurs without fanfare

When we think of historical events, especially significant ones, we think of D-Day and all the photographs, films and paintings and the world watching and holding its breath as the beaches of Normandy in France are stormed to liberate Europe from the grip of Nazi Germany. We think of Americans dumping tea into a Boston harbor and all the paintings and drawings we have seen of Americans dressed up as Indians or of Corwallis surrendering to Washington or General Lee surrendering to General Grant at Appomatox Courthouse to end five years of bloody, costly, agonizing fratricide.

But ironically, life is not always like this. A hundred and twenty five years after that Appomatox Courthouse scene and African-American men gaining the right to vote, Spartanburg County finally got around to installing its first black county magistrate in modern times. It was done in a quick moment at the county jail where the magistrates then had an office. No one thought to alert the television stations or the newspapers or if they did they didn't show up. In fact there were no dignitaries, no speeches, no bands playing.

Warren Sullivan, Jr. whose family has been in the funeral home business since 1948, one of the longest continuous businesses in that western county city, doesn't have framed pictures of the event or scrapbooks or plagues to commemorate the historic barrier-breaker. No one thought to snap a photograph or record the swearing in in any way.

The 52-year-old funeral home owner who was asked to serve as the first modern African-American magistrate in 1992, reflects from the vantage point of several decades, "It wasn't publicized. We just kind of did it and it was over. I am the kind of person who doesn't like fanfare. Just let me do my job and do it well."

"That was something historical in the area and we didn't do it right. I am not sure if it is my fault or Spartanburg County's. I can't say why it happened that way."

Sullivan had never studied the law or thought much about it or certainly not about one day being a dispenser of the law.

He had graduated from an integrated Greer High School and gone on to graduate from mortuary science at Gupton -Jones in Atlanta and had come to work in the business started by his father and two uncles.

"I had already worked at the funeral home 12 to 15 years" when he was approached about breaking the justice color barrier.

"Spartanburg County never had a black magistrate and leaders locally and in the state as a whole were putting pressure for representation. Here was Spartanburg County, one of the state's largest counties, and there was no black representation in the magistrate system."

"John McCarroll, the West Spartanburg NAACP president, was really pushing for it," Sullivan remembers, and when Glenn Reese in the Senate and Rep. Lanny Littlejohn of Whitestone pushed the idea through, McCarroll "asked me to consider it."

"You didn't need any kind of judicial background. It was more of a common sense along with the law kind of thing."

Preachers and funeral home owners are natural choices in the black community, he says, because both hold stature in the community that knows them to be honest and those who are people persons, hearing them at their highest and lowest moments.

By the time the appointment came, schools and public

accommodations in Spartanburg County had been integrated for a couple of decades.

"It was a smooth transition. Everyone assumed this was already in place and after it happened, it was like, "Wow, this just happened."

But Judge Sullivan remembers one funny incident.

Bond hearings were done at the courthouse and Judge Gowan of Reidville "was sort of my mentor" and he was there introducing the new judge around when an inmate, sort of Spartanburg County's Otis from Mayberry, a regular who drank too much, caused a disturbance and got arrested, was doing her regular thing and making noise. She was not in good enough shape to face a bond hearing at that moment. The jail said to her to be quiet and show some respect to the new judge.

"Hey, ain't no black judge in Spartanburg County," she yelled back.

But when she was properly sober and ready to face a bond hearing, she came before Sullivan in a formal way. "You're no judge," she said. He replied that he was and she said, "You mean Spartanburg County finally got a black judge?"

Sullivan, who had spent decades seeing people at their best and worst and at their highest and lowest in the funeral business, said the magistrate was not a judge looking down from the bench but was there to help rather than hurt people. "My thing was we need to be a buffer (between the big court and them being right with the law) and talk to people and to tell them how to do things right. He said he made a point to continue talking to this woman, about her life, about her drinking and about other options in life. Eventually, he said she turned her life around.

Sullivan's face lights up like a switch has been turned on when he talks about people like this.

"I was in Walmart a year ago and a man walked up to me and said, "Do you remember me? I came before you when you were a Judge. If it hadn't been for you I don't know where I would be today. You sat down and talked to me and it straightened me out."

In his three years as a part time judge, Sullivan estimates several thousand people came before him since Greer was the largest of the seven part time county magistrates, generating between

$100,000 to $150,000 a year. But he says even though this money was generated, the county wouldn't provide a secretary to the court and he had to do all his own paperwork.

All of the memories of his life on the bench are not happy ones. Crack cocaine was just starting to really come into Spartanburg County big time.

He remembers a father coming to bail his son out of jail on drug charges and in the course of talking to him found out that even though his son was only 18, the father was frightened of him. During the bond hearing the father stayed on one side of the court and the son the other and they didn't interact like most fathers and sons would. After they left to get into the father's car, he said you could hear loud talking and suddenly three or four gunshots rang out. "I was ducking down. I knew it was gunshots."

The father during the argument had ordered the son out of the car and the son grabbed the father's gun and fired at him as he sped off in the car. A deputy at the court was able to apprehend the son and Sullivan remembers sadly that only hours after doing a father's duty and bailing his son out of jail he was back at the court to sign attempted murder warrants on his own son.

Much of life's realities come to roost at the judge's doorstep. He remembers as if it was yesterday how two grown brothers in their 40s or 50s still lived with their mother who put up with the drinking son and tried to referee their fighting among themselves. Two weeks after her death, they got into a huge fight, slugging it out and finally went to their bedrooms. One brother who thought about it awhile came back to finish the argument, bringing with him a rake handle. The other brother reached for his gun and chased his brother about the house, shooting him repeatedly.

As magistrate, Sullivan couldn't set bond for this serious charge but was getting the other paperwork in order and he asked the quiet defendant, "Do you have anything to ask me." And the adult who had lost his mother and now brother in a matter of weeks said, "Yes, Judge, when can I go home?" "And I said he wasn't going to be going home anytime soon."

As a part time magistrate, Sullivan said he probably made about $1,000 a month then, but "it wasn't for the money or the prestige. I really enjoyed helping people."

Sullivan Brothers Funeral Home was started on a shoestring budget and as in any family owned business in good and bad times, money was always a consideration.

His father, Warren Sullivan Sr. and his two uncles each put in $500 after getting out of the military in World War II and began the business. His mother was a school teacher and with a regular salary, although not a lot, helped keep the family going. After a couple of years, his father found he was doing the lion's share of work at the funeral home and decided to buy out his brothers and borrowed $3,000 and gave each brother half for his interest in the business -- even though the business on South Poinsett Street still carried the name Sullivan Brothers.

Sullivan says he was adopted at the age of one from Berkeley County and says with some little choking up in his voice that he has never tried to find his birth parents. All he has known is his Sullivan family where he was an only child, but grew up with his grandparents, uncles, cousins and parents all living in four houses side by side.

His father didn't live to see him become a magistrate, dying in 1990.

"He would have been well pleased. He was a forerunner of equality. He saw segregation in World War II. He had gone through a lot of things in his life." Because black funeral homes didn't look to white people for their business, funeral home owners were able to speak their minds without any repercussions and that is why their owners across the South were able to push for equality without financial repercussions, he said.

Sullivan has two sons and a daughter and one of his sons, Maurice, has come into the business. It was the pull of the family business and the need for him to be there fulltime that caused him to give up being a magistrate after three years.

He estimates that six out of 10 defendants who came before him for civil and criminal matters were white, but he said he never heard any racial slurs, "although I don't know what they said after they left."

When he sees people out they still refer to him reverently as Judge Sullivan.

"It was a great learning experience. It was just a great

experience all the way around. I loved it. I felt like I was honest with everyone and fair with everyone. I didn't want to have to give it up but I didn't have any choice. If I wanted to keep the family business I had to devote the time to it."

Rubye Calhoun

First Black Female Magistrate

No one is ever going to accuse Rubye Calhoun of being a shrinking violet. In fact, in Southern parlance she is "a real pistol." Whether you like her or not you are not going to say you were in a room with her and didn't feel her presence or know she was there.

As Spartanburg County's first African-American female magistrate in history, she cut a swath across the legal system in a county that was late in making the court system's faces reflect the faces in the rest of the county. And in the wake of her ouster from the job she held for only several years was left some anger, bitterness, disappointment and some nagging questions about how we did business in the county.

She was not the first magistrate ousted by the county's powerful senators and will probably not be the last. No one questions the authority given to these elected officials to choose who they want to sit in that position. Even those occupying it know for sure they serve at the will and pleasure of the senators.

Supporters would say she came into the job in late 1993 seeing a system she perceived as tilted away from blacks and tried case by case to level the field, to give some breaks to those who may not have been given any breaks up to that time. They would say she didn't play the game exactly right to suit the power structure or stepped on some toes in the way she ran her court or made her decisions. Opponents would say in trying in her mind to level the playing field she tilted justice too far and gave blacks breaks or sentences lighter than she gave white citizens.

For her part she said she believes she was fair and impartial and that she let the rule of law govern even if the mother of a black defendant might later call her up and rage at her for not being more lenient. Since each case stands on its own merits and since the facts of one case may not be exactly like those of another, historians may never be able to say completely whose side was right or if the truth was somewhere in the middle.

Now a guidance counselor at the 1,700 student James F. Byrnes High School in Duncan, she seems to have put that chapter of her life behind her but can be coaxed into remembering it and remembering it with some hurt still, especially in the way she was ousted.

Appointed in late 1993 she served in that part time courthouse position until 1995 when she followed the procedure of submitting a letter to the senators asking to be reappointed. After making a little history, friends would say she hoped to make even more history by eventually being appointed the first fulltime black magistrate in modern times. But after not hearing anything from her letter she made an appointment with one of the senators to discuss her reappointment. She remembers sitting for hours to see the senator and then being told he had left, "slipping out the back door" as she puts it. She then made a call to a second senator and he began thanking her for her service in the past tense and when she pressed him, he told her she was not being reappointed.

Supporters, especially the black legislative caucus, were ready to gear up for a fight and some strategy sessions were held to decide how to bring pressure to win her reappointment.

"I was really angry about it. It may sound old-fashioned but my grandmother used to tell me, 'You are going to get upset sometimes but don't let it ruin your life.' I thought about it and asked myself was it really worth it if I was going to always be looking over my shoulder."

"I was bitter at first, but it is something you have to pray about. It may have been more hurt than bitterness, because I knew I had done everything right, had been on time, had volunteered to work more hours, help out."

She said highway patrol officers and others who dealt with her regularly would have said she was fair and impartial as she dealt mainly with traffic and domestic violence cases.

In the end, she said she may have hurt some of her supporters and friends who wanted to wage the fight to keep her in office.

But now more than 17 years later, there are little signs of her tenure in her office at Byrnes even though she said she still has a picture of her swearing in. Bright pictures and photos of her husband of 38 years and two adult children Kevin and Kimberly Odom adorn the office. She career counsels students and over the years has mentored and counseled lots of kids.

Now reflecting back she says, "When I was there I think the system was broken. I don't know if it is broken now. I think along the way the office has lost some good people because of the way it was."

"I was surprised. I guess I expected it to be somewhat fair and work as a team and be accepted. You learn life is different. It is not always fair." She said certain magistrates had their favorites and didn't like others and one magistrate could often rule the office. "I am not caught up in the hype of office. You have to be going into it for the right reason." Some of the magistrates were later exposed and got ousted or punished for wrong-doing, she said.

Born in Charlotte and raised in Greenwood, she said she never gave any thought to law enforcement or the courts or ever being involved in either.

She was working at Z.L. Madden Elementary School in charge of attendance she saw an article about the lack of education of some of the magistrates – "some didn't even have high school educations." She was walking with a friend who she walked with regularly and said she was going to ask to be considered for one of the posts. She submitted a letter and waited months until finally the appointment was made. Since it was a part time job and paid a part time salary, she worked nights and weekends and kept her regular job.

She admits that going into office she had heard all of the comments from the black community about not seeing any faces in the justice system like theirs and not getting a fair shake in the justice system.

"When I first thought of the job I mainly saw in my mind adults coming before me," she admits.

But when she saw her first young defendant brought before her in shackles, she says it really shook her. She felt a couple of tears welling up and went into her office to compose herself.

"At first it bothered me. You have to condition your mind. You didn't make that person do what they did. I have a job to do and I have to do it. I decided as long as my conscience was clear I had done all I could do."

Raised in the church in Greenwood and with a very religious grandmother, she said, "Every night before I hit the courthouse I said a little prayer to be able to go in there and do the right thing." One time she cut a young man a break if he would attend special classes and then he ended up going to none of the classes. When she issued a bench warrant for him, the youth's mother called her up and said she was angry and wouldn't talk to her for some time.

Over time she came to realize that "it is disappointing to not get a child to do what they need to do. But that person has to be self motivated to make a difference."

The two jobs have given her a unique perspective on people. At school she has seen children lost because they dropped out, including one young man who she and other mentors worked with but who dropped out of school only weeks before graduation. Now she picks up a copy of a local tabloid newspaper and now feels the hurt of seeing his picture where he has been arrested for a crime.

As a magistrate she saw the other end where they had rejected help and taken the wrong path and were now facing the punishment for the crime and she was the one charged with meting out that punishment.

What keeps you going and preventing burnout? She said the success stories, those students who drop by and say something she did or said made a difference in their lives. Sometimes you don't even realize it is important, sometimes you don't even remember the students when they come back, but she said one of the most powerful words a person trying to help others can receive are the simple words "thank you."

Schools like Byrnes have a mentoring program where adults work with students and try to guide them to the right path.

And growing up in Greenwood, Mrs. Calhoun said she certainly got this from her grandmother and from her extended family. Her mother died when she was a senior in high school and she said daily she would go into a room and cry over the loss. Her father died the year she was married and one of the most powerful people in her life, her grandmother, died the year she didn't get reappointed. "That's how I can remember the year it happened", she says.

But she said there were other adult influences in her life, her extended family of older women in the church who mentored. It was some of these teachers who sparked her interest in education.

One teacher in her church stands out. Miss Thelma Johnson, who is now deceased, had raised two children of her own but when Rubye came along, she would say to her, "That store there is having a real sale of

dresses. Go in there and pick out a couple and I will pay for them." She even helped coordinate her wedding years later.

"I had a nice and comfortable home, nothing fancy, but being around giving and caring women in church" helped mold her view of life, she said.

Religion has continued to be the rudder in her life, falling back on the hymn played at her wedding, her favorite, 'Order Your Steps,' about how you may have plans to go one way but God alters your steps and controls your life.

That is why she said she believes everything has happened in her life and moved her in God's direction for a reason and why she lives her life looking forward and not backwards.

Roberto Inclan
The first and only Hispanic-American magistrate

If you got in your car and drove from Spartanburg south all the way through Florida and on the ocean bridge all the way to Key West, a total of 715 miles, and got out of your car on the beach and looked at the ocean you would not be able to see the island nation of Cuba. It is only 90 miles from the United States but certainly a world away.

And if you were also able to transport back through time, you would see young 10-year-old Roberto Inclan riding his horse and enjoying the family ranch. But if you had told him then that he would one day have made a little history as the first Hispanic Magistrate in Spartanburg he probably either wouldn't have believed it or given any thought to it.

In fact those lawmakers in South Carolina who decades later chose him to be a magistrate probably didn't think of the significance of that selection.

Inclan, a member of a long and respected Cuban family that came to the island nation from Spain almost a century ago, ended up in a robe in Spartanburg through a chance comment and not through a methodical plan.

And when he started, it is hard to believe but he was the only person in that court who spoke Spanish. Now after his retirement the court system in the county has the availability of interpreters who make it easier to understand and work with people of other languages.

Inclan, who has a keen sense of humor, remembers his appointment. After private Catholic preparatory school, a degree from Wofford College and a law degree from the University of South Carolina, he worked in several legal positions, the longest as a lawyer for a large company, State Auto Mutual, for 28 years before it shut down its Greer division.

"I was too old to start anew but too young to fully retire," he remembers. His wife casually mentioned to the wife of his neighbor, the state senator, about her husband finding him something "to get him out of the house," he laughs.

And before you knew it, he had an appointment as a part-time magistrate's position at the courthouse, working afternoons and nights several days a week. And he worked in that position from spring of 2011 until the spring of 2018.

He says he never had any problems about defendants or others making any comments about his Hispanic heritage and was treated respectfully by most.

" I have always gotten along with everyone" and he credits this trait with getting the job done smoothly.

He said as a totally committed America, who thinks like an American, he does see a difference between himself and some Hispanics.

"I am very methodical. My legal life is based on analysis and not emotion," he says. "My judicial philosophy is justice with mercy. The under-represented deserve to be heard fully."

"I took a lot of time to make sure I got their side," he says and admits that there was "some surprise" from Hispanic visitors to the court that someone actually spoke their language.

But if he held a trial instead of the other legal matters like taking guilty pleas, he would use an interpreter to make sure everything was right.

Although Inclan has not been back to visit Cuba to visit since he fled the country as a youth, he says Cuba still recognizes him as a Cuban citizen and he is not quite sure what might happen if he showed up for a visit.

But even though it has been multiple decades since he left, he fondly remembers the country.

His grandfather, Carlos Manuel de la Torrey Gonzalez-Llorente, was chief magistrate of the Supreme Court, basically the equivalent of the U.S. Supreme Court chief justice, and served 28 years in the judiciary. Ultimately Castro swept into power and had him removed as he did with all people who served when Batista was in power. His grandfather never fled the country and lived there until he died at 73. On Jan. 1, 1959 Cuban dictator Fulgencio Batista facing the groundswell of support for Fidel Castro's 26th of July Movement, fled the island.

Inclan readily admits his view of Castro is colored by his family experience, but says the difference between Batista and Castro is "Batista wanted to get his but didn't mind if you got some too. Castro wanted to get his and didn't want anyone else to get theirs."

Inclan's stepfather had a large tobacco business and a ranch outside Havana.

Inclan was riding his horse on the ranch when two carloads of Castro's men showed up and demanded all the guns on the ranch. When he said his stepfather was sleeping, one of the men pointed a gun in the face of the 10-year-old and demanded, "Go Wake Him Up." When his awakened stepfather refused to give over the guns, the men left and soldiers showed up to confiscate the guns.

Inclan a week later fled the country with the caregiver and with only one suitcase although he admits wearing some of the family jewelry since they didn't think to frisk a preteen youngster.

He ended up living with his aunt and uncle and their eight children and the life-long care family caregiver. After graduating from a Catholic private school in Covington, Louisiana where his parents sent him to study, he returned to Tryon, N.C. where they had settled. He wanted to attend LSU like his brother but his parents told him they would pay for Wofford but not LSU, known as a party school.

Ironically he and his brother ended up at Wofford and because of the partying background at LSU, his brother graduated a half semester after Inclan.

His brother embraced his Hispanic heritage and worked in countries that spoke Spanish while Inclan fell totally in love with

America.

"America is the greatest country in the world. I love America. It is always supportive." He met his wife, the daughter of a local physician, and they moved to Columbia to start law school with only $250 in his pocket. And over the decades while he was practicing law she was teaching.

The Hispanic culture has a "less structured, happier spirit," but he said he totally embraced the more structured, organized American view of life and loved it.

His face lights up and he smiles, even grins, when he talks about his life in America, the opportunities, and his family.

And while he may not have necessarily been chosen to be a magistrate because he was Hispanic, he put his heritage, his knowledge, and his ability to speak Spanish and English to work as the county's first Hispanic judge.

CHAPTER SEVENTEEN

Chapter 17 - The Dark Side: Misconduct by Magistrates

It is unfortunate, but to give a complete picture of the history of the magistrate court, instances of inappropriate behavior by magistrates must be related. There are two types of such behavior – unethical and illegal. The first type involves actions such as the use of racial slurs or intemperance. There have been, over the years, numerous instances of judges engaged in such behavior.

After the implementation of the Judicial Reform Amendment, effective July 1, 1979, magistrates became a part of the "unified court system". What this meant was that they became subject to the disciplinary rules applicable to higher court judges. Prior to this, it is unclear what steps could be taken for magistrate's conduct short of criminal behavior. One of the earliest cases found was <u>State ex rel Lyon, Atty. Gen., T. Bowden et al</u> reported in the <u>South Carolina Reports</u> September 21, 1912, beginning at page 393. In this case, after the conclusion of the legislative session in 1911, Governor Cole Blease replaced three of Spartanburg County's magistrates, who had been appointed and confirmed, with the advice and consent of the senate, in 1909, to serve until 1911, or "until their successors were appointed and confirmed."

At the time a statute provided "Such magistrates may be suspended by the Governor for incapacity, misconduct, or neglect of duty; and the Governor shall report any suspension with the cause thereof to the Senate at the next session for its approval or disapproval." At the next session of the Senate, the suspensions were disapproved. To decide the issue, the Attorney General filed an action before the Supreme Court. The court ruled that the Governor's actions were wrong and reinstated the three original magistrates.

It is uncertain what reasons the Governor had for suspending the magistrates, but The Spartanburg Journal and Carolina Spartan newspaper in an article entitled "A Little Story on Major Kirby" dated January 9, 1915, stated " No doubt Maj. A.H. Kirby, who is in his eighty-seventh year, has been simultaneously vindicated of charges brought against him and automatically reappointed magistrate...". It is apparent that the Governor thought he had grounds to suspend the magistrate but the Supreme Court ruled that a governor, on his own, could not remove a magistrate.

Another such attempt to remove a Spartanburg magistrate occurred in 1936. The Tucapau Mill had more union members than any other textile mill in Spartanburg County. Union officers boasted membership of more than fifty percent of the workers at a time when most mills averaged about ten percent. Unions were very unpopular among mill owners. When the president of the Tucapau Mill fired two union employees for allegedly damaging a bolt of fabric the union went on strike. Violence broke out resulting in the murder of one person.

Governor Olin D. Johnston, who had grown up working in a textile mill, attempted and finally worked out a compromise to end the strike. However, after the workers returned, the mill owner began a gradual discharge of union members for various violations of work rules. Once fired, they had to vacate their mill village homes. When they refused, the mill owner decided to seek help from the magistrate court to evict them.

What happened next is recounted by Bryant Simon in his book "A fabric of defeat: the profiles of South Carolina Millhands, 1910-1948", published by UNC Press in 1998. "Magistrate R.D. Hicks of Inman served the eviction notices on the Tucapau trade unionists who had been thrown out of the mill village. This seemed strange to Governor Johnston. Why he wondered had these cases been heard in Hicks's courtroom twelve miles across rutty roads from the factory and not in the magistrate's office in Tucapau or in Spartanburg which was only ten miles away? Why, he asked, had mill officials from

Startex Mills and Spartan Mills also traveled this path?"

Professor of History at Duke University, Dr. G.C. Waldrep, III, continued the story in his book "Southern Workers and the Search for Community", published in 2000, "The Trials began in 1936. According to NLRB's (National Labor Relations Board) Feidelson, 'When the first case was tried, the magistrate refused to grant union counsel's request for a jury, did not take any evidence, and signed an order of eviction written out for him by the company attorney.' In the second trial, pro-union attorney Robert J. Gantt was able to obtain a jury, but Hicks limited the pool to eighteen local men all known for their anti-union sentiments. To everyone's surprise, even this jury – dominated by downtown merchants, textile mill supervisors, and farmers- ultimately gave a verdict for the defendant. This Hicks immediately set aside. Both cases were appealed to the county courts – one by the union - the other by the company – en route to which the official transcript of the proceedings were prepared in the Startex office by the company stenographer. An NLRB representative attended eight more evictions trials. Local 2070 attempted to mobilize the county against Hicks and obtained nearly a thousand signatures calling for his dismissal."

The <u>Spartanburg Herald</u> reported ,in an article on February 19, 1937, that Governor Olin Johnston had served a rule to show cause why he should not be removed from office on Magistrate Hicks. Three full days of hearings were conducted over two months before the governor. Allegations against the magistrate included denial of jury trials, improperly constituted jury panels, altering of the trial records sent to the appeal court, and mishandling of a charge of disruption of church worship, according to the news report. After the hearings, the governor ordered Hicks removed as a magistrate.

On March 3, 1937, the <u>Herald</u> reported, "The State Supreme Court today dismissed it's rule to show cause against Governor Olin Johnston in the appeal of R.D. Hicks, magistrate... The Governor had been cited to produce records in the trial of Hicks, who he suspended from office and who appealed his removal. In the meantime, however, the action of the Governor had been disapproved by the Senate, thus restoring Hicks to office."

Thus, it was clear as had been established twenty-five years earlier, that the governor's ability to remove a magistrate was in question. Unfortunately, the Supreme Court never had a chance to rule on the appeal. As in the earlier case of A.H. Kirby, some guidance might have been given to future governors on how to handle complaints against magistrates.

Once magistrates became part of the unified court system, their ethical conduct fell under the Judicial Code of Conduct. This consisted of a few very powerful Canons that specified proper and improper conduct for a judge. A Judicial Disciplinary Commission was set up by the Supreme Court with a disciplinary counsel who was charged with investigating and presenting cases to the Disciplinary Commission. Additionally, judges and others with questions on what behavior might run afoul of the canons could submit the questions for answers to the commission.

The disciplinary counsel was given the authority to dismiss a complaint that clearly did not set up facts that showed inappropriate behavior by a judge. Most complaints have fallen into this category over the years and have been dismissed. However, if the counsel finds grounds, he may initiate a complaint. After investigation, the complaint might be dismissed, an agreement entered into between counsel and the judge for discipline, or a contested hearing may be held. Most cases result in the agreed discipline which might result in a cautionary letter, a private reprimand, or a public reprimand. Only one complaint has ever resulted in a formal hearing. Unfortunately, this arose from Spartanburg County.

Over the years, the most common problem has been the mishandling of money. Magistrates are the only judicial officers who must receive, receipt, and transmit monies collected to the county treasurer. Even in municipal courts, there usually is a town clerk or secretary who performs these functions. Throughout history, most of the men and women who have served as magistrates have performed this function properly.

Unfortunately on occasions magistrates have been careless in the handling of funds. Sometimes this was because they did not make regular deposits. Either they would wait until a certain amount of money was collected, or they would just wait until the first opportunity to visit the bank. On one occasion a judge stopped in at the store leaving the bank deposit bag on the front seat of his unlocked car. When he returned, the bag was gone.

In several instances, the judge repaid money that was missing when there was no evidence of who, if anyone, actually stole the money. On May 25, 1950, the Spartanburg Herald-Journal reported that a Common Pleas jury awarded Spartanburg County a $1,017.58 judgment against Magistrate Ralph Mitchell for monies received between October 1-10, 1945, but that had not been paid to the county. Judge Mitchell testified that there was a long standing policy for him to leave this money at the county jail each night. He stated that bank deposits would be made 2 to 3 times weekly.

"Sheriff B.B. Brockman testified that he had given no one instructions to guard the funds which were put in a desk at the jail. He said prisoners, policemen, visitors and other persons were in the room where the money was kept. The sheriff indicated he had not been contacted about the policy of keeping the funds there.", the paper reported. The article further stated that an order had been issued by a circuit judge in the matter that "there is no charge against the magistrate of embezzlement or any other criminal act on his part. On the contrary, it was stated by the attorney for the plaintiff that he desired it clearly understood that he did not intend the action brought to even indicate any imputation of any criminal crime on the part of the defendant".

Other than paying the money, no further consequences befell the judge. Had this occurred after magistrates came under the canons, a different outcome might have occurred. On several occasions, the judge has received disciplinary action for mishandling money. In one of the most extreme cases, a chief magistrate in another county was removed as chief and later suspended by the Supreme Court for failing to properly supervise his staff. A clerk under his employ had been convicted of theft of money, and even though the judge was not implicated in the theft, the Court found that he had been forewarned of the clerk's propensity to commit theft. Accordingly, he failed to properly supervise his staff, bringing disfavor on the court.

In Spartanburg, a number of judges have been charged with theft for failing to properly receipt monies received by them. In one instance the magistrate handwrote receipts on paper grocery bags and, in another, the judge used a receipt book from a retail store. In both instances the judges had violated the order of the chief justice to provide official receipts printed by court administration. Also in both instances the judges pled guilty to theft related charges and resigned from office.

In 1978, the Spartanburg Herald reported that five magistrate offices in the state were under investigation by the State Law Enforcement Division (SLED). Most involved the mishandling of money. Two judges had resigned, one had been suspended by the Chief Justice, and other offices were closed until the investigation was complete. None of these offices was in Spartanburg. One judge allegedly had received merchandise from local merchants in exchange for his services to them and another allegedly allowed sheriff's deputies to sign his name to arrest warrants.

Attorney General Daniel McLeod was outraged, reported the paper, commenting that there were no guidelines in effect for the magistrates on handling of money. Court Administrator Edward Atwater responded by announcing a five point plan to train magistrates in proper accounting procedures. Gradually, more rules and guidelines were developed by the chief justices and court administration regarding the receipting and handling of monies coming into the courts.

In recent years, Chief Justice Toal issued a money management order setting out specific details on how judges should receive, receipt and transmit monies collected. The order requires daily deposits of funds received. In Spartanburg Chief Judge Tommy Wall had video taping equipment installed at all safes for the deposit of money. Additionally Wall instituted a checks and balances procedure where two people counted and checked all deposit bags before depositing them into the safe. Thus, today, the magistrate courts of the state are carefully scrutinized and audited to prevent mistakes in the handling of money.

Other types of misbehavior have been alleged and have unfortunately brought public disfavor on the magistrate courts. One very bizarre case was reported in The Spartanburg Herald on April 26, 1935, entitled "Floyd is Freed of One Charge". A person by the name of Ellis Guy was allowed to sign a warrant charging Magistrate W.M. Floyd with public drunkenness and public disorderly conduct. The accuser's allegations were that the judge has caused a disturbance at Hill's Café on Magnolia Street on April 21, 1935.

The article indicated that Guy called several witnesses but did not elaborate on their testimony. The case was heard by fellow Magistrate Andrew Wells. The defense attorney called a dozen witnesses who had talked with Floyd on the day of the alleged incident at his office in the courthouse. These included lawyers, police officers, and the judge's secretary. All testified he was not intoxicated but was "sober as a judge". Guy admitted on cross examination that he had been convicted of a prohibition violation.

At the conclusion of the case the judge was found not guilty on the drunkenness charge and Magistrate Wells took under advisement the disorderly conduct charge. Under today's rules a fellow magistrate would have to recuse himself from hearing such a case. The same outcome may have resulted but the canons clearly would have required a local magistrate not to hear such a case because of a conflict of interest.

Another troubling case was reported in the Spartanburg Herald-Journal on July 15, 1989 on page A1. J.D. Bruce had succeeded his father as magistrate in Lyman thirteen years earlier. A highway patrol trooper had accused the judge of offering him a $6000.00 bribe to dismiss a driving while intoxicated case. SLED was called in to investigate and found some troubling evidence in the judge's office. Chief Magistrate Edward Overcash was assigned to inventory Bruce's office. He spent several days doing this and came back frustrated at what he found.

The State Law Enforcement Division (SLED) later charged Bruce with four counts of obstruction of justice. The newspaper reported that the SLED investigation had produced no evidence of wrongdoing by anyone else. In a negotiated plea Bruce pled guilty to one count of obstruction of justice as reported by the paper. He was sentenced to ten years suspended on five years probation plus several years of house arrest according to the news report. In the August 3, 1989 edition of the same newspaper it was reported that Bruce had resigned - citing the heavy workload of the job.

In the most bizarre case in recent years, on March 23, 2005, several news outlets, including wistv.com reported "Chief Justice Jean Toal has demoted an Upstate magistrate. Johnny Cash was demoted Tuesday as Spartanburg County's chief magistrate. He remains on the bench. Toal says she thought it was appropriate to change the head of the local magistrate's court. She would not elaborate on the reasons. Toal had reappointed Cash to the position in December. " Thus began a story that rattled across the region and eventually resulted in the removal of the magistrate. Today, the case is cited at almost every seminar in which judicial misconduct is being discussed.

The removal order dated May 8, 2006, is No. 26143. Relevant portions are: " On November 2, 1991, respondent (Johnny Cash) was married. He worked as a magistrate's constable for several years, became a part-time magistrate in the late 1990's and, eventually, a full-time magistrate in 2001." The order refers to two females with whom Cash became involved as Female 1 and Female 2. "Female 1 met the respondent at the friend's house on a few occasions and, on at least one of these occasions, engaged in sexual activity. The sexual activity constituted adultery." Female 1 complained later that because of "fear of losing her job, she believed she could not refuse his advances."

"Female 2 has worked for the Magistrate Court for more than twenty years. Respondent met her while he was a constable. When he became Chief Magistrate in early 2004, respondent's supervisory responsibilities caused him to interact more frequently with Female 2.", the order continues. "Respondent acknowledges engaging in extra-marital sexual activity with Female 2 on several occasions while she was employed in the Spartanburg Magistrate Court, including on two occasions while attending court-related seminars out of town."

"On March 18, 2005, respondent's wife filed a complaint seeking a divorce from respondent on the ground of adultery. The divorce was granted by order filed August 5, 2005. Female 2 was also divorced from her husband and, subsequently, married respondent. Both continue to be employed in the Spartanburg Central Magistrate Court."

"Before respondent's romantic relationship with Female 2, but while he was the Chief Magistrate, respondent made administrative changes in the Spartanburg Central Magistrate Court that included a promotion for Female 2. Respondent contends the promotion was based exclusively on merit, experience, and longevity, but acknowledges that , in hindsight, it may have had the appearance of being based on favoritism".

The Supreme Court found that Cash had violated almost every one of the Canons of the Code of Judicial Conduct. He was ordered removed from office by every member of the Court. The ruling was reported in all the major newspapers of the state and on numerous websites such as GoUpstate.com and the South Carolina Appellate Law Blog.

Of the more than three hundred magistrates that serve in South Carolina and the hundreds who have served in the history of Spartanburg County, only a handful have run afoul of the law or engaged in ethical misconduct. However, these indiscretions are magnified by the fact that those charged with ensuring obedience to the law should abide by the same law. Failure to do so by these people undermines public confidence in the criminal justice system.

CHAPTER EIGHTEEN
Chapter 18 - Conclusion

The magistrate court of Spartanburg today is one of the most respected, if not the most respected, magistrate court in South Carolina. Our mission in writing this book was to show how that was achieved. As our history shows, there were essentially two parallel divisions of the court – the City of Spartanburg Court and the remainder of the regional district courts. The City of Spartanburg Court gradually evolved into what was referred to as the "courthouse magistrates". Later it became the Central Court.

The regional magistrates each worked on an island, seldom interacting with each other or the courthouse magistrates. Accordingly, for nearly two centuries nothing much changed in the way these magistrates went about their business. There was essentially no oversight. This, of course, led to neglect in providing adequate facilities and courtrooms or staff for these judges to receive the respect they deserved.

On the other hand, the courthouse magistrates were integrated into a legal system that was familiar to most people. They had better courtrooms, better staffing, and handled significantly more cases than their regional counterparts. Lawyers and senators, who were predominantly lawyers, felt more comfortable in this environment than they did attending court in the back room of a service station.

As a result the courthouse magistrates were transformed first in the Spartanburg Civil Courts in the mid 1950's and later in the

Spartanburg Civil and Criminal Court in 1970. There were multiple judges in the district and a chief judge that provided coordination and oversight of the district. This became the forerunner of the "central court" concept. For a quarter of a century, these courts became the face of the magistrate court system in Spartanburg. They were much more familiar to those that used the court most.

In 1979 when the Judicial Reform Amendment abolished the specialized courts and the courthouse magistrates were to be reestablished as the City of Spartanburg Magistrate Court it is understandable that the regional magistrates would eye the new district with suspicion. Even more disturbing to these judges was the new accountability and the new supervision with the creation of a chief magistrate. No longer were these judges their own bosses.

Thus the battle lines were drawn –with one faction favoring the status quo while the other sought modernization of the system. Modernization was perceived as a path to elimination of the regional magistrates by those that supported the status quo. As a result, Spartanburg was initially passed over in the creation of a central traffic court and it would be nearly ten years before traffic cases were centralized.

Once centralization began it continued to bring more and more of the functions of the court into one location. With each service that the district magistrates gave up came more fears that they would eventually be eliminated. Local senators at the time, however, stood firm in their support of the regional magistrates offices.

Thus the role of the district magistrates evolved into one of providing guidance to their local communities on remedies to their legal problems. By handling fewer trials, these judges had more time to meet with and give direction to the citizens of their communities. The district magistrates were thus part of an overall system with each judge having a clearly defined role and all working together to provide efficient judicial service to the whole community. No longer were these judges on an island alone.

Helping even more to increase the respect level of the district courts were the increased educational requirements to be a magistrate. Combined with the aptitude test to be a candidate, the certification test to determine legal knowledge, and the annual continuing education requirements, the new educational requirements helped these judges develop a higher level of judicial skills.

Spartanburg's leadership in the area of technology helped the judges develop computer literacy which further improved their efficiency. The court website, the use of the internet, and the ability to email expanded the judge's ability to better educate themselves and to provide better service to those that came before their courts.

The improved skills and knowledge of the judges combined with the spirit of comraudery among the group helped the judges avoid the pitfalls reported in the chapter on misconduct. Thus the evolution of the court has brought about greater respect from the public. Respect for the courts has led to a confidence that justice will be done in these courts.

Accordingly, those who serve in the magistrate court as judges and staff today can be proud of the new reputation. This book was written to demonstrate the path that the "people's court" took to reach this goal in Spartanburg County. A popular comedian named Rodney Dangerfield a few years back did a routine in which he claimed he "got no respect". For many years, the magistrate court was the "Rodney Dangerfield" of the court system. This is no longer true as the Spartanburg Magistrate Court has worked hard to achieve its measure of respect.

In the end the "people" in "people's court" are the winners.

CHAPTER NINETEEN
Appendicies

APPENDIX 1

Early Spartanburg County Justices of the Peace

Baylis Earle	lifetime appointment	3-24-1785
John Ford	lifetime appointment	3-24-1785
James Jorden	lifetime appointment	3-24-1785
Henry White	lifetime appointment	3-24-1785
John Thomas, Jr.	lifetime appointment	3-24-1785
William Wood	lifetime appointment	3-24-1785
Henry Macham Wood	lifetime appointment	3-24-1785
William Benson		3-4-1796

1805

John Collins and John Dean

1806

William Lipscomb, James Lucas Bird, Aaron Casey, Samuel Lancaster, John Hunter, James Drury Anderson, John Rickman, Samuel Morrow and John Walker

1807

William Lipscomb, James Lucas Bird, Aaron Casey, Samuel Lancaster, John Hunter Jones, Denney Anderson, John Rickman, Samuel Morrow and John Walker

1808

John Brewton, Daniel White, Daniel McKie, James Ford, Tyre Glenn, and Andrew Ferguson

1809

John Collins, John Dean, Henry Turner, Leonard Adcock, William Nesbitt, John Roddy, and William Reid

1810

John Hunter Jones, John Walker, Joshua Richards, Thomas Poole and

Manly Ford

1811

William Kelso, Moses Casey, John Chapman, James Hammett, Samuel Woodruff, and

John Cook

1812

John Brewton, Andrew Ferguson, Joseph Camp and

David Moore

1813

John Collins, John Deah, Henry Turner, Leonard Adcock, William Reid and

Samuel Archibald

1814

John Hunter Jones, Thomas Poole, Edward Ballenger, William Underwood and

James Hamm, Jr.

1815

William Kelso, James Hammett, Moses Casey, Samuel Woodruff, Ezekiel Dobbins,

Ephriam Lewis, John Montgomery and Caleb James

1816

James Whitten, Eaton Walker, Robert Leggon, Joseph Camp, David Moore,

Benjamin Wofford, Berry Hinds, William Hendricks and

David Lewis

William Hunter	1-4-1820
William Nelson	1-4-1820
William Bennett	1-4-1820
Caleb Jones	1-4-1820
James Whitten	1-11-1820
William Underwood	1-11-1820
Moses Casey	2-18-1820
James Brooks	2-19-1820
Ephraim Lewis	2-19-1820
J. Chapman	3-6-1820
David Mason	3-6-1820
Robert Ligard	3-6-1820
J. Montgomery	3-14-1820
J.S. Rowland	3-16-1820
Joseph Camp	3-16-1820
George Camp	3-16-1820
John Dean	6-5-1820
William Hendrix	6-5-1820
William Clement	1-1-1821
Damond Moore	1-20-1821
John Dean	2-5-1821
James Fords	2-5-1821
James Whitten	2-5-1821
Robert Ligon	2-5-1821

James B. Paslay

Ransom Foster	3-2-1821
William Young	3-5-1821
Thomas Collins	3-5-1821
Augustus Shands	6-9-1821
Joseph Wofford	1-7-1822
Tindal W. Robertson	2-14-1822
John Burns	3-4-1822
Lee Linder	3-4-1822
Joseph Camp	3-12-1822
William Smith	3-14-1822
James Foster	3-18-1822
William Dobbins	4-1-1822
Samuel Ross	4-10-1822
William Kelso	1-5-1824
William Hunt	1-7-1824
Caleb Jones	3-27-1824
David Moore	1-10-1825
John Dean	1-24-1825
James Ford	2-17-1825
William Clement	3-2-1825
Phillip Brewton	3-7-1825
William Young	3-17-1825
William Morgan	4-4-1825
Joseph Wofford	1-25-1826

Augustine Shands	2-6-1826
Joseph Camp	2-6-1826
Lee Linder	2-6-1826
J. Booker	2-6-1826
Tindal Robertson	3-6-1826
William Smith	3-11-1826
Laboy Galt	4-4-1826
Samuel Rofs	4-11-1826
Thomas Gregory	4-11-1826
Joseph W. Martin	1-13-1827
Samuel Pendant	1-13-1827
John Montgomery	2-2-1827
Ransom Foster	2-6-1827
William Bennett	3-6-1827
William Dobbins	3-6-1827
James W. Cooper	3-6-1827
Robert C. Poole	3-6-1827
E.J. Steadman	3-26-1839
Miriam White	10-6-1839
Theodore Woodruff	2-21-1840
Miriam White	3-20-1840

* * *

Appendix 2

Justices of the Quorum	Spartanburg County	
Drury McDaniel	JUSTICE of the QUORUM	1805
James Gault	JUSTICE of the QUORUM	1806
William Lancaster	JUSTICE of the QUORUM	1806
John Lipscomb	JUSTICE of the QUORUM	1806
D.J. Puckett	JUSTICE of the QUORUM	1806
William Smith	JUSTICE of the QUORUM	1807
James Gault	JUSTICE of the QUORUM	1807
William Lancaster	JUSTICE of the QUORUM	1807
John Lipscomb	JUSTICE of the QUORUM	1807
D.J. Puckett	JUSTICE of the QUORUM	1807
William Smith	JUSTICE of the QUORUM	1807
Drury McDaniel	JUSTICE of the QUORUM	1809
Samuel Morrow	JUSTICE of the QUORUM	1809
John Gossett	JUSTICE of the QUORUM	1810
John Lipscomb	JUSTICE of the QUORUM	1810
Wilson Nesbitt	JUSTICE of the QUORUM	1810
William Kelso	JUSTICE of the QUORUM	1811
Joshua Richards	JUSTICE of the QUORUM	1811
Michael Miller	JUSTICE of the QUORUM	1813
Samuel Morrow	JUSTICE of the QUORUM	1813
John Lipscomb	JUSTICE of the QUORUM	1814

Spartanburg Peoples' Court

Henry Turner	JUSTICE of the QUORUM	1814
John Chapman	JUSTICE of the QUORUM	1815
William Reid	JUSTICE of the QUORUM	1815
John Brewton	JUSTICE of the QUORUM	1816
John Collins	JUSTICE of the QUORUM	1816
Fortunatus H. Legg	JUSTICE of the QUORUM	1816
Dan White	JUSTICE of the QUORUM	1-4-1820
William Rudo	JUSTICE of the QUORUM	1-4-1820
H. Woods	JUSTICE of the QUORUM	2-29-1820
Henry Turnery	JUSTICE of the QUORUM	3-6-1820
John Lipscomb	JUSTICE of the QUORUM	3-6-1820
John Brewton	JUSTICE of the QUORUM	3-6-1820
Burnele Bobo	JUSTICE of the QUORUM	3-6-1820
James Young	JUSTICE of the QUORUM	3-6-1820
Thomas Poole	JUSTICE of the QUORUM	3-11-1820
Sam P. Archibald	JUSTICE of the QUORUM	4-11-1820
John Brewton	JUSTICE of the QUORUM	1-25-1821
James Hamm	JUSTICE of the QUORUM	2-5-1821
John Rowland	JUSTICE of the QUORUM	2-12-1821
Benjamin Wofford	JUSTICE of the QUORUM	2-5-1821
Thomas Woods	JUSTICE of the QUORUM	3-13-1821
Fortunatus H. Legg	JUSTICE of the QUORUM	1-7-1822
John Ison	JUSTICE of the QUORUM	3-18-1822
James Crook	JUSTICE of the QUORUM	3-18-1822

James B. Paslay

James Whitten	JUSTICE of the QUORUM	4-1-1822
George Camp	JUSTICE of the QUORUM	4-1-1822
James Young	JUSTICE of the QUORUM	1-17-1824
William Reid	JUSTICE of the QUORUM	1-26-1824
Daniel White	JUSTICE of the QUORUM	3-1-1824
Robert Ligon	JUSTICE of the QUORUM	4-4-1825
James Harrison	JUSTICE of the QUORUM	4-11-1825
John Burns	JUSTICE of the QUORUM	1-20-1826
Caleb Jones	JUSTICE of the QUORUM	2-6-1826
George Camp	JUSTICE of the QUORUM	2-16-1826
James Crook	JUSTICE of the QUORUM	3-6-1826
Fortunatus H. Legg	JUSTICE of the QUORUM	3-13-1826
Moses Carnes	JUSTICE of the QUORUM	3-17-1826
William Morgan	JUSTICE of the QUORUM	4-3-1826
C. Henry Turner	JUSTICE of the QUORUM	1-13-1827
John Lipscomb	JUSTICE of the QUORUM	2-2-1827
John Chapman	JUSTICE of the QUORUM	2-5-1827
John W. Harmon	JUSTICE of the QUORUM	3-24-1827

Appendix 3

Magistrate Districts Outside the City of Spartanburg in the 1800's

Magistrate Name Date	District	Appointment Date	Confirmation
P.H. Bates	Batesville		3-14-1877
B.P. Bates	Batesville		4-14-1879
R.H. Bates	Batesville		12-28-1880
B.H. Bates	Batesville		1-13-1883
N.F.B. Littlejohn	Boiling Springs		2-9-1897
M.J. McDowell	Bugerville		3-29-1879
G.E. DerBard	Cashville		3-27-1877
H.H. Arnold	Cashville		8-4-1879
G.E. Derbard	Cashville		5-23-1981
Elijah Dill	Campobello		5-31-1879
Elijah Dill	Campobello		1-1-1881
Elijah Dill	Campobello		1-21-1883
Elijah Dill	Campobello		1-13-1885
C.M. Earle	Campobello	12-28-1987	3-27-1888
Elijah Dill	Campobello	12-28-1988	2-27-1889
W.R. Tanner	Campobello		2-5-1897
John L. Poole	Campobello		6-10-1898
J.L. Poole	Campobello	2-29-1899	3-2-1899
George H. Camp	Campton		4-4-1881
George H. Camp	Campton		1-15-1885

James B. Paslay

George H. Camp	Campton	12-28-1986	2-16-1887
J.H. Camp	Campton		1-6-1891
J.H. Camp	Campton		1-5-1893
J.H. Camp	Campton		1-8-1895
W.J. McDowell	Cantrell		1-24-1885
W.J. McDowell	Cantrell	12-24-1888	1-14-1889
Thomas W. White	Cerlander		2-6-1897
J.L. Scruggs	Cherokee		3-8-1877
E.P. Epton	Cherokee	2-22-1889	3-1-1890
J.H. Oliver	Cherokee		1-22-1891
T.W. White	Clarence	2-29-1899	3-10-1899
T.P. Thackston	Clifton	2-16-1885	3-26-1887
J.G. Wardlaw	Clifton	12-28-1887	3-3-1888
J.G. Wardlaw	Clifton	12-24-1989	1-21-1890
J.G. Wardlaw	Clifton		1-12-1891
J.G. Wardlaw	Clifton		1-16-1893
J.L. Shipley	Clifton		2-5-1897
John H. Williams	Clifton		1-27-1898
J.H. Williams	Clifton	2-29-1899	3-10-1899
Alonzo Tanner	Cowpens	1-9-1883	2-7-1883
E. Potter	Cowpens		10-12-1883
Alonzo Tanner	Cowpens	1-24-1885	1886
W.R. Tanner	Cowpens	10-2-1886	10-7-1886
W.R. Tanner	Cowpens	12-27-1887	1-6-1888

E. Potter	Cowpens	1-24-1889	1-16-1890
E. Potter	Cowpens		1-6-1891
W.R. Tanner	Cowpens		12-27-1892
R.W. Lee	Cowpens		1-4-1893
R.W. Lee	Cowpens		1-7-1895
E. Potter	Cowpens	2-17-1900	2-24-1900
Miles H. Ferguson	Cross Anchor		8-25-1877
F.M. Sexton	Cross Anchor		10-9-1879
F.M. Sexton	Cross Anchor		1-11-1881
F.M. Sexton	Cross Anchor		1-22-1883
F.M. Sexton	Cross Anchor		1-16-1885
M.P. Patton	Cross Anchor	12-28-1886	1-29-1887
M.P. Patton	Cross Anchor	12-24-1888	1-16-1889
M.P. Patton	Cross Anchor		1-20-1891
B.B. Burnett	Cross Anchor		1-14-1893
M.P. Patterson	Cross Anchor		2-9-1897
M.P. Patton	Cross Anchor	2-29-1899	3-6-1899
J.P. Gaston	Duncan		1-3-1885
J.P. Gaston	Duncan	12-24 1888	1-9-1889
T.P. Gaston	Duncan		2-2-1891
J.M. Dean	Duncan	2-29-1899	3-10-1899
J.M. O'Shields	Dutchman		3-8-1895
J.M. O'Shields	Dutchman	2-9-1897	8-11-1897
J.M. Smith	Dutchman	2-29-1899	3-6-1899

James B. Paslay

Charles C. Hill	Enoree	10-14-1891	Oct. 1891
Charles C. Hill	Enoree		3-20-1896
W.A. Ray	Enoree		11-22-1897
A.B. Donald	Enoree		2-8-1898
E.B. Donald	Enoree	2-29-1899	4-7-1899
W.A.M. Dowell	Farley		1-6-1893
N.J. McDowell	Farley		12-31-1894
W.J. McDowell	Fingerville	12-28-1886	1-17-1887
J.H. Trout	Fingerville		1-17-1891
H.G. Gaffney	Gaffney		1-11-1981
Rufus G. Ray	Gaffney		3-31-1882
H.G. Gaffney	Gaffney		1-13-1882
James E. Webster	Gaffney		1-9-1885
H.G. Gaffney	Gaffney		1-12-1885
R.G. Ray	Gaffney		1-17-1885
E.P. Hollis	Gaffney	1-28-1885	1-23-1886
H.G. Gaffney	Gaffney	12-28-1886	1-13-1887
J.E. Webster	Gaffney	12-28-1886	1-14-1887
J.E. Webster	Gaffney		1-12-1891
H.G. Gaffney	Gaffney		1-12-1891
J.G. Sarratt	Gaffney		12-27-1892
J.M. Bonner	Gaffney		1-4-1893
J.G. Garrett	Gaffney		2-31-1894
William Phillips	Gaffney		12-31-1894

J.G. Sarratt	Gaffney		6-4-1897
M.W. Walker	Glendale		3-25-1898
M.W. Walter	Glendale	2-29-1899	3-6-1899
J.W. Stribling	Glenn Springs		4-3-1878
J.W. Stribling	Glenn Springs		10-28-1880
J.W. Stribling	Glenn Springs		12-30-1881
J.W. Stribling	Glenn Springs		1-9-1883
J.A.P. Lancaster	Glenn Springs		1-8-1885
J.A.P. Lancaster	Glenn Springs	12-28-1886	1-24-1887
J.A.P. Lancaster	Glenn Springs		1-12-1891
F.C. West	Glenn Springs		1-14-1891
F.C. West	Glenn Springs		12-31-1894
W.M. O'Shields	Gowensville		3-15-1877
John L. Lee	Golightly		10-12-1896
E.C. Lee	Golightly		3-11-1898
R.J. Ray	Grassy Road		1-21-1883
W.P. Thomas	Hartsville		12-28-1894
J.M. Anderson	Hillsdale		10-7-1896
W.J. Thornton	Hillsville		1-19-1895
D.B. Miles	Hobbys		1-6-1893
E.C. Clark	Inman		4-21-1892
E.C. Clark	Inman		2-17-1897
J.J. Lambright	Landrum		1-19-1883
J.J. Lambright	Landrum		1-22-1885

James B. Paslay

J.J. Lambright	Landrum	12-28-1886	2-16-1887
J.J. Lambright	Landrum		1-20-1891
J.H. Ellege	Landrum		10-18-1892
J.H. Ellege	Landrum		12-27-1892
J.H. Ellege	Landrum		12-29-1894
J.H. Ellege	Landrum		2-5-1897
Crawford Earle			2-5-1897
W.J. Lawenght	Lavarenes		10-30-1882
H.G. Gaffney	Limestone		3-9-1877
J.H. Harrison	Malwell Grove		3-8-1877
J.L. Scruggs	Martinsville		3-27-1879
J.L. Scruggs	Martinsville		1-18-1881
J.L. Scruggs	Martinsville		2-7-1883
J.L. Scruggs	Martinsville		2-13-1885
J.L. Scruggs	Martinsville	12-28-1886	2-3-1887
J.L. Scruggs	Martinsville		1-20-1891
J. Ezell	Martinsville		1-5-1893
J.J. Ezell	Martinsville		12-29-1894
J.C.L. Ezell	Martinsville		2-5-1897
H. Parris			2-5-1897
J.M. Dean	Millford		1-21-1891
B.F. Bonner	McKelveys		1-21-1881
B.F. Bonner	McKelveys		1-27-1883
J.L. Scruggs	McKelveys	12-24-1888	1-21-1889

Spartanburg Peoples' Court

R.H. Dodd	New Prospect		3-8-1877
H.J. McDowell	New Prospect		3-8-1881
G.M. Hicks	New Prospect		6-30-1897
G.M. Hicks	New Prospect	2-29-1899	3-10-1899
J.F. Sloan	Pacolet		2-8-1879
B.F. Bowen	Pacolet		6-28-1879
B.F. Bates	Pacolet	2-11-1887	2-17-1887
B.F. Bates	Pacolet	12-28-1887	1-17-1888
B.F. Bates	Pacolet		11-6-1891
B.F. Bates	Pacolet		12-27-1892
H.L.C. Murph	Pacolet		1-7-1895
B.B. James	Pacolet	6-9-1900	6-15-1900
H. Parris	Parris		1-21-1898
W. Parris	Parris	2-29-1899	3-10-1899
Miller Heines	Parris	4-20-1899	5-1-1899
W.C. Harrison	Reidville		7-25-1882
W.C. Harrison	Reidville		1-11-1883
W.C. Harrison	Reidville		1-24-1885
W.C. Harrison	Reidville	12-28-1886	1-29-1887
W.C. Harrison	Reidville	12-24-1988	1-14-1889
W.C. Harrison	Reidville		2-2-1891
W.C. Harrison	Reidville		1-11-1893
J.O. Fowler	Reidville		1-2-1895
L.M. Conner	Reidville		2-8-1897

James B. Paslay

L.M. Cannon	Reidville	2-29-1899	3-1-1899
R.A. Lancaster	Rich Hill		2-19-1885
A. Joel Foster	Rich Hill	1-24-1889	1-16-1890
A. Joel Foster	Rich Hill		1-6-1891
A. Joel Foster	Rich Hill		2-13-1893
A. Joel Foster	Rich Hill		1-7-1895
A. Joel Foster	Rich Hill		2-9-1897
H.L.C. Murph	Trough		3-31-1898
T.P. Gaston	Vernonsville		1-18-1881
T.P. Gaston	Vernonsville		1-27-1883
J.F. Harrison	Walnut Grove		5-28-1879
N.W. Bearden	Walnut Grove		6-2-1892
N.W. Bearden	Walnut Grove		3-27-1892
P.J. Deland	Wellford		3-9-1877
D.J. Finley	Wellford		3-7-1877
P.J. Deland	Wellford	12-28-1886	2-4-1887
P.J. Deland	Wellford	12-24-1888	1-21-1889
J.M. Dean	Wellford		1-5-1893
F.C. West	West Springs		1-11-1893
W.D. Chapman	Whitney P.O.		1-30-1895
A.B. Woodruff	Woodruff		3-20-1877
A.B. Woodruff	Woodruff		4-10-1879
A.B. Woodruff	Woodruff		7-28-1881
A.B. Woodruff	Woodruff		3-15-1883

A.B. Woodruff	Woodruff		3-30-1885
A.B. Woodruff	Woodruff	12-28-1886	1-26-1887
A.B. Woodruff	Woodruff	12-24-1988	1-26-1889
A.D. Chamblin	Woodruff		10-12-1891
J.B. Bragg	Woodruff		1-4-1893
J.B. Bragg	Woodruff		1-2-1895
J.B. Bragg	Woodruff		2-10-1897
J.B. Bragg	Woodruff	2-29-1899	3-1-1899

* * *

Appendix 4

Spartanburg Magistrates Between 1841 and 1900

As set out in the text magistrates began as justices of the peace and justices of the quorum. In 1841 a statute went into effect that renamed justices of the peace as magistrates and eliminated justices of the quorum. In Spartanburg magistrates were appointed only to the county and not divided into districts in the county. In the mid 1870's the county did begin dividing into magistrate districts around the county and this continues today.

For a short time from the mid 1870's until the 1895 constitution magistrates were called trial judges. This was changed back to magistrates by the new constitution. However, we refer to them all as magistrates in this book.

Magistrate Name	Date appointment confirmed
Bobo Simpson	1-26-1841
T.J. Linder	2-4-1841
Lanceford Cantrell	5-31-1841
Andrew Grambling	7-8-1841
J.B. Tolleson	3-14-1842
Robert Rogers	4-21-1842
George W.H. Legg	11-21-1842
Elias Walls	2-16-1844
W.S. Porter	3-1-1844
Moses Webber	3-11-1844
J.W. Legg	3-11-1844
K.Y. Morgan	3-11-1844
John S. Gentry	5-3-1844
H. Wofford	1-29-1845

James Smith	9-18-1845
H. G. Gaffney	7-15-1850
P.W. Head	8-14-1850
Robert Scruggs	6-16-1851
John Wheeler	4-2-1856
A.B. Woodruff	5-24-1858
J. T. Sloan	10-18-1860
Jesse Cooper	3-20-1862
Samuel Lancaster	10-30-1862
J.L. Kirby	11-23-1868
Samuel T. Passion	12-1-1868
W.M. Fleming	11-15-1869
Isaac Smith	12-24-1868
G.W. Tuck	1-6-1869
Randolph Turner	1-6-1869
A.E. Smith	1-6-1869
J.W. Wofford	1-23-1869
James T. Holt 12-9-1869	2-1-1869 removed
A.P. Turner	2-17-1869
J. Epton	2-23-1869 removed 11-10-1869
Dan G. Finley	3-1-1869
James Perry	3-9-1869

James B. Paslay

Jonas Brewton	3-11-1869
Enoch Cannon	3-24-1869
William M. Champion	3-27-1869
W.B. Carson	3-31-1869
Martin W. Glover	3-31-1869
Hiram James	4-30-1869
J.T. Walker	5-1-1869 removed 1-22-1870
Samuel Lancaster 11-10-1869	5-3-1869 removed
E. Rampley	5-11-1869
E.F. Davis	6-9-1869
Robert M. Wood	7-23-1869
Anthony Johnson	10-13-1869
Elijah Dill	11-9-1869
J.K. Staton	12-4-1869
Highlon Davis	12-16-1869
G.W.H. Legg	12-30-1869
Anthony Johnson	5-2-1870
James Perry	5-9-1870
Elijah Dill	5-17-1870
J.W. Carlisle	1-27-1871
D.R. Duncan	1-27-1871
J.W. Wofford	2-2-1871 removed

John Epton	2-4-1871 removed
J.C. Foster	2-7-1871 removed
William Irwin	2-7-1871
W.H. Montgomery	2-14-1871
W.C. Camp	3-2-1871
D.G. Finley	3-10-1871 removed
W.J. Parker	4-8-1872
J.W. Tuck	4-18-1872
W.M. Fleming	4-23-1872
B.F. Bates	6-6-1872
J.B. Tolleson	1-17-1873
B.F. Bates	1-15-1873
J.R. Johnson	1-15-1873
H.G. Gaffney	3-12-1873
W.F. Parker	3-15-1873
B.F. Bates	4-26-1873 removed 6-10-1874
C.C. Turner	4-28-1873
M.M. Glover	4-30-1873
G.W. Tuck	5-1-1873
E.P. Clement	5-2-1873
Samuel T. Aromis	1-3-1874
R.A. Pralis	3-25-1874 removed 5-8-1874
Samuel T. Aromis	3-25-1874

James B. Paslay

B.J. Bates	3-27-1874 removed 6-10-1874
H.H. Glover	4-2-1874
B.J. Parker	4-8-1874
G.W. Tuck	4-3-1874
C.C. Turner	4-3-1874
E.P. Clement	4-4-1874
M.C. Hubbard	5-14-1874
J.J. Morro	5-15-1874
B.H. Steadman	7-8-1874
Alexander Jones	8-20-1874
B.F. Balis	10-9-1874
A.B. Woodruff	3-18-1875
G.E. DeBand	5-5-1975
G.W. Tuck	10-30-1876
A.C. Merrick	10-30-1876
Alexander Jones	2-3-1875
William Invier	2-3-1875
B.J. Bates	2-5-1875
J.B. Tolleson	2-8-1875
Elijah Dill	2-8-1875
C.C. Turner	2-8-1875
H.W. Foster	2-8-1875
H.G. Gaffney	2-8-1875

H.J. Parker	2-10-1875
D.R. Thomason	2-10-1875
Harvey Wofford	2-13-1875
H.G. Fairley	2-17-1875
H.H. Scaif	1-30-1877
George H. Legge	1-30-1877
D.G. Finley	3-3-1877
A.C. Merrick	7-3-1877
W.J. McDowell	3-20-1878
H.G. Gaffney	2-26-1879
J.T. McCravy	6-30-1880
J.W. Elford	12-30-1881
W.S. Thomason	1-8-1881
P.J. Deland	1-10-1885
W.P. Elford	1-14-1885 resigned 4-22-1885
A.B. Garland	4-27-1885
A.B. Garland	1-19-1886 resigned 3-21-1887

City of Spartanburg District established

Judge's name	Date appointed	Date confirmed
H.E. Ravenel	12-31-1886	1-4-1887

James B. Paslay

T.B. Thackston	3-26-1887	3-31-1887
T.B. Thackston	12-28-1887	1-7-1888
H.E. Ravenel	12-28-1887	1-7-1888 resigned 5-1-1888
Howard B. Carlisle	12-28-1887	6-25-1888 resigned 2-1-1889
J.E. Webster	12-24-1888	1-8-1889
H.G. Gaffney	12-24-1888	1-9-1889
F.C. West	12-24-1888	1-10-1889
J.H. Camp	12-24-1888	1-11-1889
George H. Hinnant	2-5-1889	2-8-1989 resigned 7-20-1890
T.B. Thackston	1-24-1889	1-16-1890
J.F. Gates	1-10-1890	2-15-1890
J.J. Burnette	7-26-1890	7-26-1890
A.H. Kirby		1-8-1891
William W. Johnson		1-15-1891 resigned 12-22-1891
L.E. Farley		12-24-1891 resigned 9-30-1892
J.J. Gentry		10-3-1892
A.H. Kirby		1-6-1893
J.W. Nash		10-9-1894
J.N. Nash		12-20-1894
A.H. Kirby		12-31-1894
J.M. Dean		1-3-1895
G.C. Clark		1-3-1895
A.B. Layton		1-3-1895

J.L. Shippy		1-3-1895
J.N. Shields		3-8-1895
W.G.S. O'Shields		3-3-1896
A.H. Kirby		2-4-1897
W.G.S. O'Shields		2-5-1897
W.M. Anderson		3-19-1897 resigned 11-17-1897
A.H. Kirby	2-29-1899	3-1-1899
P.H. McGowan	2-29-1899	3-1-1899

* * *

Appendix 5
Spartanburg District Magistrates since 1900

Judge Name	District	Appointed	Confirmed
W.W. Wood	Arlington	18-Jan-07	24-Jan-07
J.F. Henderson	Arlington	05-Feb-09	10-Feb-09
J.F. Henderson	Arlington	08-Feb-131	7-Feb-13
J.F. Henderson	Arlington	08-Feb-15	12-Feb-15
J.F. Henderson	Arlington	20-Feb-17	26-Feb-17
O.R. McCarter	Arlington	30-Jan-29	16-Feb-29
O.R. McCarter	Arlington	25-Feb-31	05-Mar-31
N.F.B. Littlejohn	Boiling Springs	############	
W.T.B. Littlejohn	Boiling Springs	20-Feb-04	29-Feb-04
W.T.B. Littlejohn	Boiling Springs	20-Feb-05	07-Mar-05
J.C.L. Turner	Boiling Springs	14-Feb-06	20-Feb-06
Charlie Hughes	Boiling Springs	27-May-58	11-Jun-58
S. Frank Adams	Boiling Springs	10-Jun-92	24-Jun-92
S. Frank Adams	Boiling Springs	16-Jun-95	19-Jun-95
S. Frank Adams	Boiling Springs	24-Aug-2001	13-Sep-2001
S. Frank Adams	Boiling Springs	21 May 2019	5 Jul 2019
Teresa Ledbetter	Boiling Springs	2 Apr 2014	11 Apr 2014
Teresa Ledbetter	Boiling Springs	21 May 2019	5 Jul 2019
W.R. Tanner	Campobello	##############	
John L. Poole	Campobello	##############	
John L. Poole	Campobello	##############	
John L. Poole	Campobello	09-Feb-01	14-Feb-01
John L. Poole	Campobello	20-Feb-03	24-Feb-03
D.H. Golightly	Campobello	20-Feb-03	02-Mar-03
John L. Poole	Campobello	20-Feb-05	25-Feb-05
B.B. Chapman	Campobello	18-Jan-07	25-Jan-07
J.L. Poole	Campobello	24-Jan-07	30-Jan-07
J.L. Poole	Campobello	05-Feb-09	10-Feb-09
B.B. Chapman	Campobello	05-Feb-09	15-Feb-09
J.L. Poole	Campobello	20-Feb-11	24-Feb-11
B.B. Chapman	Campobello	20-Feb-11	04-Mar-11
J.L. Poole	Campobello	08-Feb-13	13-Feb-13
J.L. Poole	Campobello	08-Feb-15	12-Feb-15
J.L. Poole	Campobello	20-Feb-17	26-Feb-17
J.L. Pool	Campobello	15-Feb-19	18-Feb-19
J.L. Pool	Campobello	04-Mar-21	08-Mar-21
L.F. Wall	Campobello	14-Jul-22	17-Jul-22
L.F. Wall	Campobello	01-Mar-23	19-Mar-23
L. F. Wall	Campobello	24-Feb-25	21-Mar-25
L.F. Wall	Campobello	21-Mar-27	28-Mar-27
L.F. Wall	Campobello	30-Jan-29	04-Mar-29

L.F. Wall	Campobello	25-Feb-31	04-Apr-31
Lewis F. Wall	Campobello	23-Jun-4	30-Jun-42
Lewis F .Wall	Campobello	17-Mar-43	09-Apr-43
J.J.C. Ezell	Cherokee	18-Jan-07	28-Jan-07
W.L. Ezell	Cherokee	17-Mar-09	22-Mar-09
L.H. Williams	Cherokee	20-Feb-11	24-Feb-11
T.F. Henderson	Cherokee	20-Dec-12	26-Dec-12
T.F. Henderson	Cherokee	08-Feb-13	12-Feb-13
J.J.C. Ezell	Cherokee	04-Mar-21	10-Mar-21
Zeno Blackwell	Chesnee	20-Feb-11	24-Feb-11
John Belton Cash	Chesnee	14-Jul-11	18-Jul-11
A.C. Wall	Chesnee	02-Jan-12	05-Jan-12
K.D. Edwards	Chesnee	02-Jan-14	06-Jan-14
J.J. O. Exell	Chesnee	08-Feb-15	13-Feb-15
J.J.C. Ezell	Chesnee	20-Feb-17	02-Mar-17
J.J.C. Ezell	Chesnee	01-Mar-23	16-Mar-23
W.H. Wall	Chesnee	24-Feb-25	18-Mar-25
Grady W. Lee	Chesnee	21-Mar-27	24-Mar-27
J.H. Cash	Chesnee	15-Feb-29	25-Feb-29
J.F. Ezell	Chesnee	24-Jan-30	27-Jan-30
Elias F. Wall	Chesnee	04-Feb-32	06-Feb-32
E.F. Wall	Chesnee	15-Mar-33	28-Mar-33
E.F. Wall	Chesnee	28-Apr-36	29-Apr-36
J.H. Garrison	Chesnee	11-Jul-40	17-Jul-40
E.F. Wall	Chesnee	18-Mar-41	22-Mar-41
E.F. Wall	Chesnee	17-Mar-43	23-Mar-43
Frank C. Robbins	Chesnee	02-Jul-48	07-Jul-48
Frank C. Robbins	Chesnee	25-Apr-53	22-May-53
Frank C. Robbins	Chesnee	05-Jul-56	09-Jul-56
Frank Robbins	Chesnee	17-Jul-58	24-Jul-58
Frank C. Robbins	Chesnee	13-Jul-60	28-Jul-60
Frank C. Robbins	Chesnee	09-Jul-62	19-Jul-62
Jack Cantrell	Chesnee	10-Dec-63	13-Dec-63
W. Lynn Watson	Chesnee	16-Dec-64	06-Jan-65
Walter Lynn Watson	Chesnee	14-Dec-66	30-Dec-66
Walter Lynn Watson Jr.	Chesnee	28-Jan-69	12-Feb-69
Walter Lynn Watson	Chesnee	08-Feb-73	17-Apr-73
Mrs. Kathryn Watson	Chesnee	25-Jun-75	23-Jul-75
Kathryn Watson	Chesnee	26-Jan-77	14-Feb-77
Benny Fagan	Chesnee	01-Mar-78	09-Mar-78
Benny Fagan	Chesnee	20-Feb-81	06-Apr-81
Frank C. Robbins	Chesnee	13-Oct-82	21-Oct-82
MaxRoss	Chesnee	26-Mar-85	01-Apr-85
Larry M. Hutchins	Chesnee	28-May-87	08-Jun-87
Larry M .Hutchins	Chesnee	10-Jun-92	19-Jun-92
Harold W. Pryor	Chesnee	08-Jun-95	21-Jun-95
Larry M. Hutchins	Chesnee	08-Jun-95	19-Jun-95
Johnny L. Cash	Chesnee	23-May-98	29-May-98
Johnny L. Cash	Chesnee	24-May-99	07-Jun-99

James B. Paslay

John Amick Morrow	Chesnee	02-Mar-2001	13-Mar-2001
Daniel R. Burns	Chesnee	14-Apr-2006	24-Apr-2006
Daniel T. Burns	Chesnee	7 Apr 2009	22 Apr 2009
Edward Addington	Chesnee	30-Apr-2011	
Edward Addington	Chesnee	2-Apr-2014	9-Apr-2014
Edward Addington	Chesnee	21 May 2019	Jul 5 2019
Thomas W. White	Clarence	##############	
T.W. White	Clarence	##############	
C.C. Bearden	Clarence	09-Feb-01	16-Feb-01
D.H. Golightly	Clarence	18-Feb-02	25-Feb-02
F.L. Shipley	Clifton	############	
John H. Williams	Clifton	###########	
E. Potter	Clifton	15-Jul-05	18-Jul-05
J.H. Williams	Clifton	23-Mar-48	07-Jun-48
DuPre Vaughn	Clifton	17-Jul-58	24-Jul-58
J.H. Williams	Converse	20-Feb-03	24-Feb-03
J.H. Williams	Converse	24-Sep-36	28-Sep-36
J.H. Williams	Converse	27-May-40	14-Jun-40
J.H. Williams	Converse	05-Oct-42	12-Oct-42
DuPre Vaughn	Converse	06-Jan-49	12-Jan-49
DuPre Vaughn	Converse	11-Jun-52	16-Jn-52
Dupre Vaughn	Converse	05-Jul-56	09-Jul-56
Dupre Vaughn	Converse	13-Jul-60	27-Jul-60
DuPre Vaughn	Converse	09-Jul-62	01-Aug-62
John W. Fortune	Converse	09-Oct-64	21-Oct-64
John W. Fortune	Converse	14-Dec-66	27-Dec-66
John W. Fortune	Converse	28-Jan-69	08-Feb-69
John W. Fortune	Converse	08-Feb-73	01-Mar-73
John W. Fortune	Converse	26-Jan-77	09-Feb-77
John W. Fortune	Converse	20-Feb-81	09-Mar-81
John W. Fortune	Converse	26-Mar-85	08-Apr-85
E. Potter	Cowpens	18-Feb-00	25-Feb-00
E. Potter	Cowpens	09-Feb-01	14-Feb-01
E. Potter	Cowpens	20-Feb-03	24-Feb-03
E. Potter	Cowpens	20-Feb-0 5	24-Feb-05
E. Potter	Cowpens	18-Jan-07	23-Jan-07
E. Potter	Cowpens	05-Feb-09	08-Feb-09
W.R. Tanner	Cowpens	20-Feb-11	28-Feb-11
J.B. Addison	Cowpens	08-Feb-13	13-Feb-13
T.B. Addison	Cowpens	18-Apr-13	21-Apr-18
E. Potter	Cowpens	08-Feb-15	11-Feb-15
E. Potter	Cowpens	20-Feb-17	26-Feb-17
E. Potter	Cowpens	15-Feb-19	18-Feb-19
C.L. Hammett	Cowpens	04-Mar-21	08-Mar-21
E. Potter	Cowpens	01-Mar-23	12-Mar-23
E. Potter	Cowpens	24-Feb-25	18-Mar-25
E. Potter	Cowpens	21-Mar-27	24-Mar-27

E. Potter	Cowpens	30-Jan-29	04-Feb-29
E. Potter	Cowpens	25-Feb-31	28-Feb-31
M.R. Cash	Cowpens	23-Jun-42	27-Jun-42
M.R. Cash	Cowpens	17-Mar-43	26-Mar-43
M.R. Cash	Cowpens	09-Jun-49	14-Jun-49
Roy C. Cash	Cowpens	02-Apr-54	09-Apr-54
M.P. Patton	Cross Anchor	############	
M.P. Patton	Cross Anchor	############	
M.P. Patton	Cross Anchor	09-Feb-01	14-Feb-01
M.P. Patton	Cross Anchor	20-Feb-03	27-Feb-03
M.P. Patton	Cross Anchor	20-Feb-05	24-Feb-05
Hiram Yarborough	Cross Anchor	18-Jan-07	08-Feb-07
H. Yarborough	Cross Anchor	05-Feb-09	20-Feb-09
H. Yarborough	Cross Anchor	20-Feb-11	10-Apr-11
S.D. Watson	Cross Anchor	10-Oct-12	13-Oct-12
C.D. Watson	Cross Anchor	08-Feb-13	18-Feb-13
C.D. Watson	Cross Anchor	08-Feb-15	31-Mar-15
C.D. Watson	Cross Anchor	20-Feb-17	02-Mar-17
C.D. Watson	Cross Anchor	27-Feb-19	18-Mar-19
Wister L. Poole	Cross Anchor	05-Mar-20	07-May-20
J.R. Snoddy	Cross Anchor	01-Mar-23	14-Mar-23
John Franklin	Cross Anchor	24-Feb-25	21-Mar-25
J.R. Franklin	Cross Anchor	21-Mar-27	30-Mar-27
J.R. Franklin	Cross Anchor	15-Feb-29	08-Mar-29
G.C. Templeton	Cross Anchor	22-May-31	28-May-31
J.M. Dean	Duncan	##################	
J.M. Dean	Duncan	##################	
J.M. Dean	Duncan	09-Feb-01	14-Feb-01
J.M. Dean	Duncan	20-Feb-03	26-Feb-03
J.M. Dean	Duncan	20-Feb-05	24-Feb-05
J.M. Dean	Duncan	18-Jan-07	07-Feb-07
J.M Dean	Duncan	05-Feb-09	12-Feb-09
W.C. Harrison	Duncan	19-Feb-10	04-Mar-10
J.M. Dean	Duncan	20-Feb-11	23-Feb-11
J.M. Dean	Duncan	08-Feb-13	17-Feb-13
T.W. Moore	Duncan	08-Feb-15	11-Feb-15
W.C. Harrison	Duncan	08-Feb-15	13-Feb-15
F.W. Moore	Duncan	20-Feb-17	26-Feb-17
W.C. Harrison	Duncan	20-Feb-17	28-Mar-17
F.H. Moore	Duncan	15-Feb-19	18-Feb-19
W.C. Harrison	Duncan	15-Feb-19	24-Feb-19
J.O. Hendrix	Duncan	30-Jan-29	15-Feb-29
J.O. Hendrix	Duncan	25-Feb-31	11-Mar-31
F.Walker Moore	Duncan	24-Feb-38	25-Feb-38
Fred Moore	Duncan	07-Jul-39	12-Jul-39
J.M. Drummond	Duncan	14-Mar-42	21-Mar-42
Fred Moore	Duncan	17-Mar-43	06-Apr-43
Fred Moore	Duncan	17-Mar-44	27-Mar-44
Jesse M. Kennedy	Duncan	08-Mar-52	12-Mar-52

Jesse M. Kennedy	Duncan	05-Jul-56	12-Jul-56
W.M. Jones	Duncan	06-Feb-61	16-Feb-61
A.W. Ertzberger	Duncan	16-Dec-64	23-Dec-64
Artemis W. Ertzberger	Duncan	14-Dec-66	27-Dec-66
J.M. O'Shields	Dutchman	##############	
J.M. Smith	Dutchman		
####################			
John M. Smith	Dutchman	09-Feb-01	18-Feb-01
John M. Smith	Dutchman	20-Feb-03	03-Mar-03
J.M. Smith	Dutchman	20-Feb-05	27-Feb-05
John M. Smith	Dutchman	18-Jan-07	24-Jan-07
John M. Smith	Dutchman	05-Feb-09	20-Feb-09
Charles C. Hill	Enoree	###############	
W.A. Ray	Enoree	###############	
E.B. Donato	Enoree	###############	
E.B. Donald	Enoree	###############	
E.B. Donald	Enoree	24-May-02	02-Jun-02
E.B. Donald	Enoree	20-Feb-03	13-Mar-03
T.A. Simmons	Enoree	11-Apr-04	20-Apr-04
T.A. Simmons	Enoree	20-Feb-05	06-Apr-05
T.A. Simmons	Enoree	05-Feb-09	19-Feb-09
T.A. Simmons	Enoree	20-Feb-11	28-Feb-11
J.H. Waldrop	Enoree	05-Feb-14	10-Feb-14
J.L. Waldrop	Enoree	08-Feb-15	12-Feb-15
J.L. Waldrop	Enoree	20-Feb-17	26-Feb-17
J.L. Waldrop	Enoree	15-Feb-19	24-Feb-19
J.L. Waldrop	Enoree	04-Mar-21	10-Mar-21
C.D. Watson	Enoree	04-Mar-21	10-Mar-21
J.L. Waldrop	Enoree	01-Mar-23	08-Jun-23
W.F. O'Shields	Enoree	13-Sep-24	22-Sep-24
W.F. O'Shields	Enoree	24-Feb-25	25-Mar-25
J.L. Waldrop	Enoree	24-Feb-25	20-Apr-25
J.L. Waldrop	Enoree	21-Mar-27	28-Mar-27
J.L. Waldrop	Enoree	30-Jan-29	06-Feb-29
W.M. Carter	Enoree	25-May-29	28-May-29
W.M. Carter	Enoree	15-Mar-33	20-Mar-33
W.M. Carter	Enoree	23-Apr-35	29-Apr-35
W.M. Carter	Enoree	03-Mar-35	13-Mar-35
W.M. Carter	Enoree	14-Mar-42	19-Mar-42
W.M. Carter	Enoree	17-Mar-43	20-Mar-43
W.M. Carter	Enoree	30-Mar-48	01-Apr-48
J. Harold Stoner	Enoree	11-Jan-50	06-Jan-50
J. Harold Stoner	Enoree	25-Apr-53	01-May-53
P.C. Turner	Enoree	05-Jul-56	09-Jul-56
Harold Stoner	Enoree	17-Jul-58	21-Jul-58
Harold Stoner	Enoree	13-Jul-60	22-Jul-60
Harold Stoner	Enoree	09-Jul-62	17-Jul-62
Harold Stoner	Enoree	16-Dec-64	23-Dec-64
Harold Stoner	Enoree	14-Dec-66	27-Dec-66

James Harold Stoner	Enoree	28-Jan-69	11-Feb-69
James Harold Stoner	Enoree	08-Feb-73	05-Mar-73
James Harold Stoner	Enoree	26-Jan-77	09-Feb-77
James Harold Stoner	Enoree	20-Feb-81	02-Mar-81
J. Harold Stoner	Enoree	26-Mar-85	01-Apr-85
W.L. Hope Sr.	Fairforest	05-Jul-56	09-Jul-56
W. L. Hope	Fairforest	17-Jul-59	01-Aug-58
H.T. Hope Sr.	Fairforest	13-Jul-60	07-Sep-60
W.F. Hope Sr.	Fairforest	09-Jul-62	06-Aug-62
Jerry W. Morgan	Fairforest	22-Jul-64	28-Jul-64
Jerry W. Morgan	Fairforest	14-Dec-66	11-Jan-67
Jerry Wilber Morgan	Fairforest	28-Jan-69	08-Feb-69
Loyd Tipton	Fairforest	16-Jan-73	01-Feb-73
Loyd Tipton	Fairforest	26-Jan-77	23-Feb-77
Loyd Tipton	Fairforest	20-Feb-81	26-Feb-81
Loyd Tipton	Fairforest	26-Mar-85	09-Apr-85
J.G. Sarratt	Gaffney		
#########################			
M.W. Walker	Glendale		
#########################			
W.M. Walker	Glendale		
#########################			
M.W. Walker	Glendale	09-Feb-01	14-Feb-01
M.W. Walker	Glendale	20-Feb-03	24-Feb-03
S.M. Bagwell	Glendale	20-Feb-04	29-Feb-04
S.M. Bagwell	Glendale	20-Feb-05	27-Feb-05
J.H. Williams	Glendale	18-Jan-07	26-Jan-07
J.H. Williams	Glendale	05-Feb-09	09-Feb-09
J.H. Williams	Glendale	20-Feb-11	25-Feb-11
Z.W. Vandiver	Glendale	08-Feb-13	13-Feb-13
J.H. Williams	Glendale	08-Feb-15	12-Feb-15
J.H. Williams	Glendale	20-Feb-17	26-Feb-17
J.H. Williams	Glendale	15-Feb-19	18-Feb-19
J.H. Williams	Glendale	04-Mar-21	10-Mar-21
J.H. Williams	Glendale	01-Mar-23	22-Mar-23
John L. LeMaster	Glendale	24-Feb-25	18-Mar-25
John L. LeMaster	Glendale	21-Mar-27	24-Mar-27
J.J. Fowler	Glendale	15-Feb-29	22-Feb-29
Joe J. Fowler	Glendale	25-Feb-31	28-Feb-31
J.C. LeMaster	Glendale	13-May-36	15-May-36
J.C. LeMaster	Glendale	05-May-38	11-May-38
J.C. LeMaster	Glendale	01-May-40	03-May-40
J.J. Fowler	Glendale	12-Oct-42	15-Oct-42
J.C. LeMaster	Glendale	17-Mar-43	23-Mar-43
J.C. LeMaster	Glendale	06-Apr-48	13-Apr-48
J.C. LeMaster	Glendale	25-Apr-53	19-Jun-53
Walter L. Gregory	Glendale	17-Nov-53	12-Jan-54
J.A.P. Lancaster	Glenn Springs	13-Feb-09	19-Feb-09
J.A.P. Lancaster	Glenn Springs	20-Feb-11	04-Mar-11

James B. Paslay

J.A.P. Lancaster	Glenn Springs	08-Feb-13	25-Feb-13
J.A.P. Lancaster	Glenn Springs	20-Feb-17	03-Mar-17
John C. Lee	Golightly	###############	
J.C. Lee	Golightly	###############	
M.M. Bradshaw	Greeleyville	01-Nov-20	06-Nov-20
W.W. Wood	Greer	14-Feb-06	21-Feb-06
J.F. Henderson	Greer	20-Feb-11	27-Feb-11
W.W. Wood	Greer	20-Feb-18	28-Feb-18
L.H. Mayfield	Greer	05-Mar-20	15-Mar-20
L.H. Mayfield	Greer	04-Mar-21	23-Mar-21
James Stewart	Greer	22-Jun-21	20-Jul-21
R.R. Dempsey	Greer	13-Sep-21	19-Sep-21
R.R. Dempsey	Greer	01-Mar-23	19-Mar-23
R.R. Dempsey	Greer	24-Feb-25	17-Mar-25
R.R. Dempsey	Greer	21-Mar-27	25-Mar-27
Roy L.Lister	Greer	28-Aug-34	01-Sep-34
O.C. Dobson	Greer	18-May-37	21-May-37
C.B. Rollins	Greer	14-Mar-42	19-Mar-42
W.Ennis James	Greer	02-Apr-54	13-Apr-54
W.Ennis James Jr.	Greer	05-Jul-56	20-Jul-56
Jeff D. Brown	Greer	08-Jul-58	15-Jul-58
Jeff G. Brown	Greer	13-Jul-60	22-Jul-60
Jeff G. Brown	Greer	09-Jul-62	19-Jul-62
Jeff G. Brown	Greer	16-Dec-64	23-Dec-64
Jeff G. Brown	Greer	14-Dec-66	27-Dec-66
Jeff G. Brown	Greer	28-Jan-69	04-Feb-69
Jeff G. Brown	Greer	08-Feb-73	28-Feb-73
Jeff G. Brown	Greer	26-Jan-77	11-Feb-77
Harold N. Brown	Greer	26-Mar-81	06-Apr-81
Harold N. Brown	Greer	26-Mar-85	01-Apr-85
Warren H. Sullivan,Jr	Greer	10-Jun-92	24-Jun-92
Donnie B. Blackley	Greer	08-Jun-95	19-Jun-95
Donnie B. Blackley	Greer	24-May-99	29-Jun-99
Ben Johnson	Greer	19 Jun 2013	5 Jul 2013
J.M. Anderson	Hillsville	############	
Evins V. Lanford	Hobbysville	19-Feb-15	02-Mar-15
E.C. Clark	Inman	##############	
E.C. Clark	Inman	09-Feb-01	20-Feb-01
E.C. Clark	Inman	18-Feb-02	24-Feb-02
B.B. Bishop	Inman	06-Feb-03	06-Feb-03
B.B. Bishop	Inman	20-Feb-05	24-Feb-05
D.H. Golightly	Inman	20-Feb-05	04-Mar-05
W.J. McDowell	Inman	18-Jan-07	22-Jan-07
D.H. Golightly	Inman	18-Jan-07	24-Jan-07
W.J. McDowell	Inman	18-Jan-07	04-Feb-07
W.T. Bragg	Inman	13-Aug-07	20-Aug-07
D.H. Golightly	Inman	05-Feb-09	09-Feb-09
W.T. Baggott	Inman	05-Feb-09	10-Feb-09
T.B. Moore	Inman	20-Feb-11	24-Feb-11

W.J. McDowell	Inman	20-Feb-11	04-Mar-11
Charlie Mitchell	Inman	30-May-12	04-Jun-12
Charlie Mitchell	Inman	08-Feb-13	19-Feb-13
S.H. Culbreth	Inman	16-Dec-13	18-Dec-13
T.M. Hicks	Inman	08-Feb-15	01-Mar-15
R.D. Hicks	Inman	25-Feb-31	02-Mar-31
J.M. Hicks	Inman	25-Feb-31	03-Mar-31
W.F. Baggett	Inman	08-Feb-15	11-Feb-15
W.F. Baggatt	Inman	20-Feb-17	03-Mar-17
G.M. Hicks	Inman	20-Feb-17	09-Mar-17
G.M. Hicks	Inman	15-Feb-19	28-Feb-19
R.D. Hicks	Inman	27-Feb-19	03-Mar-19
R.D. Hicks	Inman	04-Mar-21	10-Mar-21
G.M. Hicks	Inman	01-Mar-23	15-Mar-23
R.D. Hicks	Inman	01-Mar-23	19-Mar-23
R.D. Hicks	Inman	24-Feb-25	18-Mar-25
G.M. Hicks	Inman	24-Feb-25	21-Mar-25
JohnHarley	Inman	21-Mar-27	28-Mar-27
G.M. Hicks	Inman	21-Mar-27	05-Apr-27
R.D. Hicks	Inman	21-Mar-27	06-Apr-27
R.D. Hicks	Inman	30-Jan-29	04-Feb-29
G.M. Hicks	Inman	30-Jan-29	06-Feb-29
J.R. Harley	Inman	15-Feb-29	25-Feb-29
R.D. Hicks	Inman	25-Feb-31	02-Mar-31
G.M. Hicks	Inman	25-Feb-31	03-Mar-31
J.H. Ballenger	Inman	20-Apr-33	25-Apr-33
R.D. Hicks	Inman	23-Apr-35	29-Apr-35
R.D. Hicks	Inman	27-May-40	14-Jun-40
R.D. Hicks	Inman	14-Mar-42	25-Mar-42
R.D. Hicks	Inman	17-Mar-43	20-Mar-43
Robert E. Lyda	Inman	02-Sep-48	28-Sep-48
C.Y. McDowell	Inman	14-Mar-49	24-Mar-49
R.D. Hicks	Inman	27-Sep-51	01-Oct-51
Thomas E. Culp	Inman	05-Jul-56	10-Jul-56
J.A. Taylor	Inman	19-Mar-57	21-Mar-57
Jonas O. Taylor	Inman	09-Jul-62	19-Jul-62
Jonas Taylor	Inman	16-Dec-64	23-Dec-64
Jonas A. Taylor	Inman	14-Dec-66	27-Dec-66
O. Manning Edwards	Inman	22-Jan-69	29-Jan-69
Edgar Lee Marlowe	Inman	23-Jan-73	05-Feb-73
O. Manning Edwards	Inman	08-Feb-73	06-Apr-73
O. Manning Edwards	Inman	26-Jan-77	09-Feb-77
O. Manning Edwards	Inman	20-Feb-81	04-Mar-81
O. Manning Edwards	Inman	26-Mar-85	15-Apr-85
Kenneth H. Dover	Inman	10-Jun-92	24-Jun-92
Kenneth H. Dover	Inman	08-Jun-95	19-Jun-95
Kenneth H. Dover	Inman	24-May-99	21-Jun-99
Kenneth Dover 2012	Inman	2 May 2012	22 May

Alton Kimbrell	Inman D 11	17-Jul-58	23-Jul-58
Fred V. Seay	Inman D 11	13-Jul-60	20-Jul-60
Fred V. Seay	Inman D 11	09-Jul-62	17-Jul-62
Fred V. Seay	Inman D 11	16-Dec-64	23-Dec-64
Fred Victor Seay	Inman D 11	14-Dec-66	27-Dec-66
Fred Victor Seay	Inman D 11	28-Jan-69	06-Mar-69
John Earl Lee	Inman D 11	24-Aug-70	04-Sep-70
John E. Lee	Inman D 11	03-Feb-71	08-Feb-71
Edgar L. Marlowe	Inman D 11	26-Jan-77	07-Feb-77
GaryRobertson	Inman D 11	30-Mar-78	30-Mar-78
GaryRobertson	Inman D 11	20-Feb-81	06-Mar-81
Joe Harold Hill	Inman D 11	28-May-81	10-Jun-81
Joseph Wayne Pugh	Inman D 11	27-Nov-81	10-Dec-81
Russell Lathan	Inman D 11	06-Mar-86	10-Mar-86
J.H. Elledge	Landrum	###############	
E.C. Fain	Landrum	20-Feb-04	03-Mar-04
J.H. Elledge	Landrum	10-Aug-04	20-Aug-04
J.H. Elledge	Landrum	20-Feb-05	24-Feb-05
T.D. Earle	Landrum	18-Jan-07	23-Jan-07
E.M. Merritt	Landrum	12-Feb-07	14-Feb-07
C.M. Steadman	Landrum	12-Feb-07	15-Mar-07
C.M. Steadman	Landrum	05-Feb-09	09-Feb-09
C.M. Steadman	Landrum	20-Feb-11	24-Feb-11
W.L. Sanders	Landrum	8-Feb-13	13-Feb-13
W. Harry Dorill, Jr.	Landrum	10-Mar-13	15-Mar-13
J.H. Randolph	Landrum	05-Oct-14	09-Oct-14
J.E. Bullington	Landrum	08-Feb-15	12-Feb-15
C.M. Steadman	Landrum	14-Oct-15	19-Oct-15
C.M. Steadman	Landrum	20-Feb-17	26-Feb-17
C. Cantrell	Landrum	19-Jun-17	22-Jun-17
C. Cantrell	Landrum	15-Feb-19	24-Feb-19
C. Cantrell	Landrum	04-Mar-21	10-Mar-21
A.D. Truette	Landrum	23-Oct-23	29-Oct-23
A.M. Foster	Landrum	24-Feb-25	18-Mar-25
Charles J. Stover	Landrum	30-Jul-28	10-Aug-28
Charles O. Smith	Landrum	15-Feb-29	22-Feb-29
A.J. Caldwell	Landrum	09-Nov-29	16-Nov-29
W.R. Dillingham Jr.	Landrum	15-Mar-33	28-Mar-33
W.R. Dillingham Jr.	Landrum	23-Apr-35	07-May-35
C.M. Steadman	Landrum	26-Mar-36	31-Mar-36
C.M. Steadman	Landrum	05-May-38	09-May-38
C.M. Steadman	Landrum	02-Feb-40	05-Feb-40
C.M. Steadman	Landrum	17-Mar-43	20-Mar-43
J.M. Byrd	Landrum	08-Apr-49	14-Apr-49
J.M. Byrd	Landrum	25-Apr-53	05-May-53
J.M. Byrd	Landrum	05-Jul-56	12-Jul-56
J. Mike Byrd	Landrum	17-Jul-58	24-Jul-58
J. Mike Byrd	Landrum	13-Jul-60	20-Jul-60
J.M. Byrd	Landrum	09-Jul-62	17-Jul-62

J. Mike Byrd	Landrum	16-Dec-64	23-Dec-64
Joseph Michael Byrd	Landrum	14-Dec-66	27-Dec-66
Joseph Michael Byrd	Landrum	28-Jan-69	05-Feb-69
Mrs. Inez B. Byrd	Landrum	10-Aug-70	17-Aug-70
Leonard E. Smith	Landrum	03-Feb-71	05-Feb-71
Leonard E. Smith	Landrum	08-Feb-73	08-Mar-73
Leonard E. Smith	Landrum	26-Jan-77	14-Mar-77
Leonard E. Smith	Landrum	20-Feb-81	06-Mar-81
Leonard E. Smith	Landrum	26-Mar-85	09-Apr-85
James F. Ashmore	Landrum	10-Jun-92	19-Jun-92
James F. Ashmore	Landrum	05-Jun-95	19-Jun-95
James F. Ashmore	Landrum	24-May-99	07-Jun-99
John M. Rollins	Landrum	14-Jun-2001	29-Jun-2001
Tina McMillan	Landrum	14 Jan 2010	22 Jan 2010
Tina McMillan	Landrum	3 Mar 2011	19 Apr 2011
W. Herbert Groce	Lyman	30-Jan-29	12-Feb-29
Charlie Eubanks	Lyman	09-Jul-62	17-Jul-62
Charlie Eubanks	Lyman	28-Jan-69	11-Feb-69
J.C. Bruce	Lyman	31-Oct-72	06-Nov-72
J.C. Bruce	Lyman	08-Feb-73	05-Mar-73
James D. Bruce	Lyman	14-Jan-77	27-Jan-77
James D. Bruce	Lyman	20-Feb-81	03-Apr-81
James D. Bruce	Lyman	26-Mar-85	01-Apr-85
J.J.C.Ezell	Martinsville	###############	
J.L. Berry	Moore	20-Feb-03	27-Feb-03
J.L. Berry	Moore	20-Feb-05	04-Apr-05
J.L. Berry	Moore	18-Jan-07	11-Feb-07
J.L. Berry	Moore	05-Feb-09	15-Feb-09
J.L. Berry	Moore	20-Feb-11	01-Mar-11
E.H. Lanford	Moore	06-Jan-13	11-Jan-13
O.W. Harrison	Moore	08-Feb-13	17-Feb-13
E.H. Lanford	Moore	08-Feb-13	19-Feb-13
T.S. Harrison	Moore	15-Feb-19	25-Feb-19
F. S. Harrison	Moore No.2	21-Mar-27	28-Mar-27
G.M. Hicks	New Prospect	#############	
G.M. Hicks	New Prospect	#############	
George M. Hicks	New Prospect	09-Feb-01	06-Mar-01
G.M. Hicks	New Prospect	20-Feb-03	26-Feb-03
John L. McWhorter	New Prospect	20-Feb-04	29-Feb-04
J.L. McWhorter	New Prospect	20-Feb-05	07-Apr-05
B.B. Chapman	New Prospect	15-Jul-05	22-Jul-05
James W.Tribble	New Prospect	04-Mar-21	21-Mar-21
B.B. James	Pacolet	09-Jun-00	15-Jun-00
D.T. Gossett	Pacolet	18-Jan-07	23-Jan-07
D.F. Gossett	Pacolet	05-Feb-09	11-Feb-09
J.L. Brown	Pacolet	08-Feb-13	14-Feb-13
D.T. Gossett	Pacolet	08-Feb-15	13-Feb-15
D.T. Gossett	Pacolet	03-Mar-35	10-Mar-35
Vernon A. Brown	Pacolet	18-Jun-38	20-Jun-38

James B. Paslay

V.A. Brown	Pacolet	15-Jan-40	19-Jan-40
F.O. Tate	Pacolet	09-Mar-42	11-Mar-42
Vernon A. Brown	Pacolet	13-Aug-47	25-Aug-47
James H. Greene	Pacolet	29-Feb-52	04-Mar-52
James H. Greene	Pacolet	05-Jul-56	09-Jul-56
James H. Greene	Pacolet	17-Jul-58	21-Jul-58
Roy Kirby	Pacolet	13-Jul-60	23-Jul-60
Roy Kirby	Pacolet	09-Jul-62	11-Sep-62
William A. Millwood	Pacolet	16-Dec-64	02-Jan-65
William H. Millwood	Pacolet	14-Dec-66	20-Dec-66
Jesse D. Allen	Pacolet	18-May-67	02-Jun-67
H. Maulden Pearson	Pacolet	06-Nov-67	13-Nov-67
H. Maulden Pearson	Pacolet	28-Jan-69	04-Feb-69
H. Maulden Pearson	Pacolet	08-Feb-73	07-Mar-73
H. Maulden Pearson	Pacolet	26-Jan-77	09-Feb-77
H. Maulden Pearson	Pacolet	20-Feb-81	11-Mar-81
H. Maulden Pearson	Pacolet	26-Mar-85	08-Apr-85
H. Maulden Pearson	Pacolet	10-Jun-92	24-Jun-92
Jimmy B. Henson	Pacolet	16-Jun-95	26-Jun-95
Jimmy B. Henson	Pacolet	24-May-99	14-Jun-99
Jimmy B. Henson	Pacolet	24 Feb 2010	17 Mar 2010
J.B. Greer	Pacolet Mills	30-Jan-29	04-Feb-29
F.O. Tate	Pacolet Mills	23-Jun-45	26-Jun-45
H. Parris	Parris	#############	
H. Parris	Parris	#############	
Miller Hines	Parris	#############	
Miller Hines	Parris	09-Feb-01	16-Feb-01
M. Hines	Parris	20-Feb-03	09-Mar-03
M. Hines	Parris	20-Feb-05	02-Mar-05
J. Walter West	Pauline	18-Jan-07	24-Jan-07
J. Walter West	Pauline	05-Feb-09	10-Feb-09
J. Walter West	Pauline	20-Feb-11	23-Feb-11
John M. Smith	Pauline	20-Feb-11	27-Feb-11
J.M. O'Shields	Pauline	08-Feb-13	17-Feb-13
J.L.M. Williams	Pauline	20-Feb-17	26-Feb-17
J.L.M. Williams	Pauline	15-Feb-19	18-Feb-19
S.S. Pettit	Pauline	04-Mar-21	10-Mar-21
John L. Lancaster	Pauline	22-Mar-21	29-Mar-21
Sam L.Strange	Pauline	01-Mar-23	13-Mar-23
S.S. Pettit	Pauline	01-Mar-23	15-Mar-23
Sam L.Strange	Pauline	24-Feb-25	21-Mar-25
M.C. Thomas	Pauline	21-Mar-27	28-Mar-27
J.A.P. Lancaster	Pauline	30-Jan-29	04-Feb-29
J.A.P. Lancaster	Pauline	17-Sep-32	26-Sep-32
Alan E.Lawson	Pauline	05-Jul-56	09-Jul-56
Allen E. Lawson	Pauline	17-Jul-58	25-Jul-58
Allen E. Lawson	Pauline	13-Jul-60	26-Jul-60
W.E. Sellers	Pauline	17-Nov-60	17-Nov-60
D.H. Leonard	Pelham	09-Feb-01	14-Feb-01

D.H. Leonard	Pelham	20-Feb-03	02-Mar-03
T.W. Wood	Pelham	15-Dec-03	30-Dec-03
W.W. Wood	Pelham	20-Feb-05	16-Mar-05
L.M. Conner	Reidville	################	
L.M. Cannon	Reidville	################	
F.O. Fowler	Reidville	09-Feb-01	14-Feb-01
R.L. Pearson	Reidville	18-Jan-07	26-Jan-07
R.L. Pearson	Reidville	05-Feb-09	11-Feb-09
T.O. Fowler	Reidville	20-Feb-11	27-Feb-11
S.E. Hendrix	Reidville	08-Feb-13	17-Feb-13
S.E. Hendrix	Reidville	04-Mar-21	10-Mar-21
S.E. Hendrix	Reidville	01-Mar-23	20-Mar-23
S.E. Hendrix	Reidville	24-Feb-25	18-Mar-25
S.E. Hendrix	Reidville	21-Mar-27	30-Mar-27
S.E. Hendricks	Reidville	21-May-37	04-Jun-37
S.E. Hendrix	Reidville	27-May-40	14-Jun-40
A.C. Gaston	Reidville	12-Oct-42	17-Oct-42
J.O. Hendrix	Reidville	17-Mar-43	31-Mar-43
J.O. Hendrix	Reidville	25-Apr-53	05-May-53
J.O. Hendrix	Reidville	05-Jul-56	18-Jul-56
J.O. Henrix	Reidville	17-Jul-58	15-Aug-58
J.O. Hendrix	Reidville	13-Jul-60	09-Aug-60
J.O. Hendrix	Reidville	09-Jul-62	09-Oct-62
J.O. Hendrix	Reidville	16-Dec-64	05-Jan-65
J.O. Hendrix	Reidville	14-Dec-66	30-Dec-66
H.M. Coggins	Reidville	03-Feb-71	08-Feb-71
Harold M. Coggins	Reidville	08-Feb-73	02-Mar-73
Harold M. Coggins	Reidville	26-Jan-77	11-Feb-77
George Floyd	Reidville	09-Nov-77	16-Nov-77
George Floyd	Reidville	20-Feb-81	03-Apr-81
George Floyd	Reidville	26-Mar-85	09-Apr-85
Eber C. Gowan	Reidville	9-Sep-89	28-Sep-89
Eber C. Gowan	Reidville	10-Jun-92	19-Jun-92
Eber C. Gowan	Reidville	08-Jun-95	21-Jun-95
David C. Snow	Reidville	12-Jun-96	28-Jun-96
Eber C. Gowan	Reidville	24-May-99	07-Jun-99
David C. Snow	Reidville	24-May-99	09-Jun-99
James H. West, II	Reidville	29 Oct 2009	4 Nov. 2009
A.J. Foster	Rich Hill	#############	
E.C. Daniel	Roebuck	30-Jan-29	06-Feb-29
Robert J. Harrison	Roebuck	07-Mar-61	18-Mar-61
Robert J. Harrison	Roebuck	09-Jul-62	27-Jul-62
D.A. Davis	Roebuck	16-Dec-64	23-Dec-64
Dempsie A. Davis	Roebuck	14-Dec-66	27-Dec-66
David O. Hawkins	Roebuck	03-Feb-71	05-Feb-71
David O. Hawkins	Roebuck	07-Feb-73	22-Feb-73
J.D. Smith	Roebuck	26-Mar-75	17-Apr-75
Ernest D. Martin	Roebuck	14-Jan-77	27-Jan-77
Ernest D. Martin	Roebuck	20-Feb-81	06-Mar-81

Q. Michael Wood	Roebuck	07-May-84	08-May-84
Q. Michael Wood	Roebuck	26-Mar-85	15-Apr-85
W.C. O'Shields	Startex	17-Jul-58	23-Jul-58
W.C. O'Shields	Startex	13-Jul-60	02-Aug-60
H.L.C. Murph	Trough	############	
D.T. Gossett	Trough	09-Feb-01	14-Feb-01
D.T. Gossett	Trough	20-Feb-03	02-Mar-03
D.T. Gossett	Trough	20-Feb-05	25-Feb-05
S.S. Tiner	Trough	20-Feb-11	22-Feb-11
J.B. Morris	Trough	20-Feb-17	02-Mar-17
T.G. Chaen	Trough	27-Feb-19	05-Mar-19
D.T. Gossett	Trough	04-Mar-21	10-Mar-21
D.T. Gossett	Trough	01-Mar-23	14-Mar-23
D.T. Gossett	Trough	24-Feb-25	17-Mar-25
D.T. Gossett	Trough	21-Mar-27	25-Mar-27
W.C. O'Shields	Tucapau	04-Mar-21	10-Mar-21
W.C. O'Shields	Tucapau	01-Mar-23	16-Mar-23
W.C. O'Shields	Tucapau	24-Feb-25	18-Mar-25
W.C. O'Shields	Tucapau	21-Mar-27	24-Mar-27
W.D. Smith	Tucapau	30-Sep-31	06-Oct-31
W.C. O'Shields	Tucapau	11-May-33	20-May-33
W.C. O'Shields	Tucapau	23-Apr-35	29-Apr-35
W.C. O'Shields	Tucapau	23-Jun-37	25-Jun-37
James E. Powell	Valley Falls	05-Jul-56	10-Jul-56
W.A. Bruce	Wellford	08-Jul-13	22-Jul-13
W.A. Bruce	Wellford	08-Feb-15	13-Feb-15
W.A. Bruce	Wellford	20-Feb-17	26-Feb-17
W.A. Bruce	Wellford	15-Feb-19	27-Feb-19
W.A. Bruce	Wellford	04-Mar-21	10-Mar-21
W.A. Bruce	Wellford	01-Mar-23	15-Mar-23
W.A. Bruce	Wellford	24-Feb-25	18-Mar-25
S.W. Dobson	Wellford	11-May-62	11-May-62
J.A.P. Lancaster	Whitestone	15-Feb-19	03-Mar-19
J.A.P. Lancaster	Whitestone	04-Mar-21	10-Mar-21
J.A.P. Lancaster	Whitestone	01-Mar-23	19-Mar-23
J.A.P. Lancaster	Whitestone	24-Feb-25	28-Mar-25
J.A.P. Lancaster	Whitestone	21-Mar-27	28-Mar-27
C.M. Bissell	Whitney	05-Feb-09	11-Feb-09
J.B. Farrow	Whitney	17-Sep-09	23-Sep-09
J.B. Farrow	Whitney	20-Feb-11	21-Mar-11
James B. Farrow	Whitney	08-Feb-13	20-Feb-13
J.B. Bragg	Woodruff	#############	
J.B. Bragg	Woodruff	#############	
J.B. Bragg	Woodruff	20-Feb-03	03-Mar-03
J.B. Bragg	Woodruff	20-Feb-05	10-Mar-05
J.B. Bragg	Woodruff	18-Jan-07	22-Jan-07
J.B. Bragg	Woodruff	05-Feb-09	11-Feb-09
J.B. Bragg	Woodruff	20-Feb-11	27-Feb-11
J.E. Exell	Woodruff	21-Mar-12	26-Mar-12

J.M Gray	Woodruff	12-Oct-12	13-Oct-12
J.M. Gray	Woodruff	08-Feb-13	12-Feb-13
J.B. Bragg	Woodruff	08-Feb-13	17-Feb-13
A.D. Chamblin	Woodruff	08-Feb-15	12-Feb-15
A.D. Chamblin	Woodruff	20-Feb-17	07-Mar-17
A.D. Chamblin	Woodruff	15-Feb-19	24-Feb-19
J.M. Gray	Woodruff	04-Mar-21	10-Mar-21
J.M. Gray	Woodruff	01-Mar-23	14-Mar-23
J.M. Gray	Woodruff	24-Feb-25	21-Mar-25
J.M. Gray	Woodruff	21-Mar-27	06-Apr-27
H.B. Crow	Woodruff	30-Jan-29	01-Feb-29
W.B. Alexander	Woodruff	15-Mar-33	18-Mar-33
H.B. Crow	Woodruff	23-Apr-35	29-Apr-35
H.B. Crow	Woodruff	27-May-40	14-Jun-40
B.D. Alexander	Woodruff	23-Jun-42	26-Jun-42
B.D. Alexander	Woodruff	17-Mar-43	31-Mar-43
R.L. Robinson	Woodruff	17-Feb-47	24-Feb-47
R.L. Robinson	Woodruff	25-Apr-53	12-May-53
J.C. Gray	Woodruff	08-Dec-53	14-Dec-53
J.C. Gray	Woodruff	05-Jul-56	09-Jul-56
Carlisle J. Gray	Woodruff	17-Jul-58	23-Jul-58
J.C. Gray	Woodruff	13-Jul-60	22-Jul-60
J.C. Gray	Woodruff	09-Jul-62	17-Jul-62
Mrs. Mozell C. Gray	Woodruff	11-Mar-64	19-Mar-64
J. Frank Wesson	Woodruff	16-Dec-64	23-Dec-64
Bryan McAbee	Woodruff	14-Dec-66	19-Dec-66
Raymond P. Cox	Woodruff	03-Feb-71	08-Feb-71
Raymond P. Cox	Woodruff	08-Feb-73	12-Apr-73
Raymond P. Cox	Woodruff	26-Jan-77	11-Apr-77
Raymond P. Cox	Woodruff	20-Feb-81	06-Mar-81
Raymond P. Cox	Woodruff	26-Mar-85	08-Apr-85
Vickie R.M. Smith	Woodruff	10-Jun-92	22-Jun-92
Vickie R.M. Smith	Woodruff	08-Jun-95	26-Jun-95
Vickie R.M. Smith	Woodruff	24-May-99	14-Jun-99
Vickie R.M. Smith	Woodruff	7 Apr 2009	24 Apr 2009
Vickie R.M. Smith	Woodruff	25 Mar 2011	19 Apr 2011
Vickie R.M. Smith	Woodruff	21 May 2019	5 Jul 2019

APPENDIX 6

Spartanburg County's Courthouses

Following are the courthouses from beginning until the present.
Some pictures are based on descriptions found when no photo or
Drawing of the building could be found.

The First Courthouse

Prior to 1785 there were no formal courts in the upstate. In 1785 Judge Pendleton's "County Court Act" was passed. This created the Spartan District into an independent district. Seven Justices of the

Peace were given lifetime appointments for the district on March 24, 1785. These were Baylis Earle, John Ford, James Jorden, John Thomas, Jr., Henry White, Henry M. Wood and William Wood. This is the only time in history that judges have received lifetime appointments.

Three of the judges were to hold court in the district every three months. However, the only location for the courts was in the home of plantation owners. These justices actually established the government of the district by appointing a sheriff and other officials and appointing the first attorney in the district.

Disputes began to occur as to what plantations to meet in, so on December 18, 1786, the justices decided to find a permanent location for a courthouse and set out in early 1787 to find a location. After searching around the district including areas like present day Boiling Springs and unable to agree they settled for the night in early 1787 at the location of the present Daniel Morgan statute on Morgan Square in the present city of Spartanburg.

After a long night of drinking they agreed to choose this location for the courthouse. In early February, 1787, a builder was chosen and a plan settled on for the structure.

The building would be a log cabin 30 feet long by 20 feet. A courtroom with an elevated jury room as well as an elevated judge's bench and witness chair would be included. Behind the building would be another log cabin for a jail (called goal at the time).

Several drawings of the building have appeared in Dr. J.B. O. Landrum's book "History of Spartanburg County" and in the Spartanburg Herald Journal newspaper a number of times.

Spartanburg's Second Courthouse

Not much is known about the second courthouse authorized by the General Assembly In 1825, begun in 1826, and occupied in 1827. It was built at the same location as the first courthouse on Morgan Square about where the Daniel Morgan statue is today.

It is reported to have been a beautiful building two stories high covered in whitewashed stone. The lower floor contained offices and the upper floor had the courtroom and jury rooms.

Since no photos or drawings exist showing the building an artist rendering is above depicting building similarities to buildings of its era in time.

Courthouse 3

"In 1856 a new courthouse was begun, on the site of the old one, which was demolished in three weeks, beginning May 12. Efforts were made to secure the preservation of the old one as a town hall, but in vain. The contract for this third courthouse was awarded by the commissioners to Maxwell and Bost, for $13,000 and the old building. Most present-day Spartans are familiar with the appearance of this courthouse, as shown in the picture of "The Square in 1884". The building was of brick with a brick colonnade in front, the pillars coated with white plaster. The offices were on the ground floor, and the second floor was occupied by the courtroom and jury rooms. Wide stone steps with curving iron railing led from the street to each side of the upper floor." Quote from WPA book.

Courthouse 4

The fourth courthouse was completed in 1896 and appears in many photos and picture postcards. It's location was moved to Magnolia Street at the present intersection with St. John St. a block from Morgan Square. It was a beautiful structure which still stood when I was a young man. I remember following my father around inside the building and up and down spiral stairways and across the black and white checkerboard tile floor. Across the street today still remains the Cleveland Law Range which was built of similar brick materials.

Behind the courthouse was the jail. In the early days the magistrate court was in the basement of the courthouse. In later years when room in the courthouse became more limited the magistrate court was moved to a small block building in the middle of the rear parking lot of the current courthouse.

The building was allowed to stand for a few years but finally was knocked down. The building did not want to go and there were stories in the local press of the difficulty destroying the building.

Courthouse 5

The current courthouse was completed in 1956. It began with prisoners from the attached jail breaking out with a spoon. This happened twice in two weeks because the bars had not been properly cemented in.

The building seemed alright for about the first twenty years but began a series of serious problems. The windows leaked every time it rained. There was a shelf under the windows where books and records were stored for several years. After the leaking began this could no longer happen.

The building leaked into the basement offices where the magistrate court resided because no leaking protection had been installed in the front of the building that was underground. It took several efforts to correct this problem.

The HVAC system installed on the roof was supposed to be cleaned every year but it was learned that it was built in such a way that maintenance had not been done in twenty seven years.

It was not until a high court judge found black mold in his office and courtroom that the public learned of the problems with the building. Efforts to fix the problems caused many employees to complain that they were being made sick by such efforts.

Once the press got involved and continued to report these problems county government allowed a vote to raise the sales tax one cent to pay for a new courthouse. Surprisingly and happily this bill passed.

As this book is being sent to press the new building is underway.

Bibliography

1. "History of Spartanburg County" by J.B.O. Landrum
The Franklin Prtg. And Pub. Co., Atlanta, GA   1900
2. "A History of Spartanburg County" compiled by the Spartanburg
Unit of the Writers Program of the WPA in S.C. Band and White 1940
3. "Vogues in Villany: Crime and Retribution in Ante-Bellum South Carolina
by Jack Kenny Williams. University of S.C. Press. Columbia 1959
4. "The Colony of South Carolina"   by Nanci A. Lyman . Franklin Watts, Inc.
New York . 1975
5. "South Carolina: A Synoptic History for Laymen" by Lewis P. Jones. 1975
6. " A Pictorial History of Spartanburg County" by Phillip Racine. Donnig Company
Publishers, Virginia Beach, VA. 1980
7. "Our Heritage" by the Spartanburg Herald Journal, Inc. 1983
8. "Spartanburg: Facts, Reminiscenses, Folklore" by Vernon Foster and Walter S. Montgomery, Sr. The Spartanburg County Foundation   1998
9. "Law and People in Colonial America" by Peter Charles Hoffer
The Johns Hopkins University Press , Baltimore Maryland

1998
10. "Southern Workers and the search for Community: Spartanburg County, South Carolina" by G.C. Waldrep III – University of Illinois Press 2000
11. "The history of South Carolina under the proprietary government, 1670-1719" by Edward McCrady, MacMillen Company 1897
12. " The Law of Magistrates and Constables in the State of South Carolina" by B.C. Pressley, Walker and Burke Publishing 1848
13. "The history of South Carolina under the royal government, 1719-1776" By Edward McCrady, MacMillen Company 1899
14. "The South Carolina Regulators" by Richard Maxwell Brown, Belnap Press 1963

Made in the USA
Columbia, SC
02 May 2024